29

Black & White:
A Survivor's Story
THIRD EDITION

– RENÉE MATTHEWS –

To Nicola with love from Renée xxx Jan 2014 xxx

An environmentally friendly book printed and bound in England by
www.printondemand-worldwide.com

Mixed Sources
Product group from well-managed
forests, and other controlled sources
www.fsc.org Cert no. TT-COC-002641
© 1996 Forest Stewardship Council
FSC

PEFC Certified
This product is
from sustainably
managed forests
and controlled
sources
www.pefc.org
PEFC
PEFC/16-33-415

This book is made entirely of chain-of-custody materials

www.fast-print.net/store.php

Black & White: A Survivor's Story
Third Edition
Copyright © Renée Matthews 2013

A catalogue record for this book is available from the British Library

ISBN 978-178035-763-8

First published 2013 by
FASTPRINT PUBLISHING
Peterborough, England.

Contents

Black & White – 'A Survivor's Story' is a memoir and a true story. The events depicted in it are, therefore, real and backed up by written reports from the British Metropolitan Police Force, Social Services departments and statements from witnesses. All the names in this book are real, apart from Steppy and Miss Elle, which were changed for personal reasons. A few anecdotes were also injected to enliven certain events but without destroying the integrity and essence of the story.

Dedication

To my mother's younger sister, Auntie Florence and her family, the 'Iyen-Omagbons' of Connecticut, the United States of America, I dedicate this book. Without your timely visit, divine intervention and unconditional love for me, my precious Auntie, I would be nothing but a mere skeleton in a grave by now. My kindest regards to your other half, our wonderful Uncle Pelas, for welcoming Jamie and I into your humble abode. Both of you not only supported us, but also helped boost my self-confidence, which renewed my zest for life. Your wise counsel gave me the courage to *'Confront My Pharaoh',* after which I was strong enough to move on. That phrase *(invented by you),* is my secret weapon for dealing with obstacles and it shall never be forgotten! I have nothing but the greatest respect, admiration, appreciation and love for you and your entire family. Rest assured that your time and effort lavished on us shall not be in vain. You are the reason I am alive to write this book and I thank you all from the bottom of my heart!

Synopsis

Black & White – 'A Survivor's Story', is an intriguing and compelling true story about living with, and eventually breaking free from an emotionally and physically abusive relationship.

The author Renée Matthews gives an amazing account of her love for a man who certainly did not turn out to be her prince charming, but instead, a *frog* of the worse kind; *an abuser*. As a result, his atrocious treatment of her, provided her with her very own domestic violence story.

Having spent years trying to keep her abusive relationship under wraps, she finally took the plunge to free herself. This happened after her husband had not only threatened to kill her, but also boasted he could get away with the crime. For her, that was the final straw! She decided not to wait to find out whether he meant to carry out his threat or not. Crushed by grief, she eventually fled to the United States with her only son, aged three.

Due to her personal experiences, she is able to highlight the effects of her circumstances to raise awareness of domestic violence and how it affects people's lives.

Renée's narrative of her emotional roller-coaster experience is heart wrenching. However, there is a twist to her tale that changed everything...

Black & White –
A Survivor's Story

Chapter One:
Welcome To England

'Oh, how cold!' I muttered to myself, shivering as I walked towards the exit of the plane to embrace the chilly air. The aircraft's staircase had been unfurled to create a door that was now wide open, and as I walked closer, it got colder. I could feel my whole body begin to tremble at this strange new life spread out before me.

What do I do? How can I possibly endure this unkind weather that is so cold and bitter? As I wondered, deep within me a sense of panic kept gnawing away and I got lost in my thoughts as I carried on walking.

Suddenly, I stopped for a moment, moving aside to allow the passengers behind me to pass through, while at the same time sifting through the contents of my handbag. After a brief rummage, I found what I was looking for and held on to it tightly, while double-checking to ensure my two small bags were still held firmly in each hand.

'Thank you for flying Nigerian Airways.' One of the flight attendants near the door said in a deep baritone voice as he leaned forward, smiling. The freezing weather was still fresh in my mind, however, I could not help but notice that he was young, tall, dark and handsome. I smiled back, mumbled a 'thanks to God for the safe flight,' and then moved on.

The realisation that I was now completely helpless against the ravages of the harsh weather forced me to brace myself. As I proceeded to alight from the plane, the stiff bitter wind slapped me, face first, welcoming me to England.

'Jeez', I sighed, shrugging my shoulders as my feet hit the ground. Almost running, I quickly moved on, following in the direction of the other passengers walking through the cold aerobridge to the terminal building.

I was shuddering and shaking like a leaf, but still wobbling ahead regardless. The weather was so ferocious it was unbearable, and I stopped for a minute to wrap my flimsy scarf around my neck properly. A little warmer, I swapped the bags round that I was holding in each hand. Immediately, I noticed that my arms, which were covered in goose bumps, resembled those of someone badly ravaged by measles. *'Nawa o!'* I sighed, mouthing a Pidgin English word native to Nigeria, often used as an exclamation or surprise.

Feeling the frozen solid air and cold go straight through to my very bones, I carried on, though, trembling very badly. 'Lord, have mercy!' I thought out loud. *I was beginning to feel like the living dead.*

★ ★ ★

It was 1989. I was coming back to London from Nigeria after a 17-year absence. Silly me; wearing only a sleeveless top and a little wrap around skirt with a matching scarf, was nothing short of foolishness and ignorance on my part.

Having left London, my place of birth, at the very tender age of five, I was mostly accustomed to the dry, hot weather in Africa. I never remembered, nor did it occur to me that I was to encounter the severe British weather, wintry even in October.

The sad fact is that I am always prone to cold conditions. Believe you me, I often wore jumpers even when the weather was mild in Nigeria. Had I not known, for most of my life, only the excessive heat of Africa, I would never have dreamt of wearing such light clothing to this frozen land. I had to resign myself to the ordeal, which was self-inflicted indeed. It was punishment for my lack of research into the British weather prior to my journey.

My Mum left Nigeria to work in London two years earlier and Gloria, my immediate younger sister, joined her there one year later after finishing her secondary education. I had not spoken to my mum or sister in the past six weeks and they probably, must have forgotten to warn me. Perhaps, in their opinion, the weather may not have seemed as unbearably cold for them as it was for me.

★ ★ ★

For me, it was still shank's pony. I felt numb and barely able to move. I began to feel and look so tired that one would think I had done the whole stretch from Nigeria to London on foot.

On reaching the terminal building, I noticed the directions to the Arrivals Hall were well signposted, which was a relief. With my eyes glued to the arrivals signs, I strolled along the walkway and I thought I could hear the walls of Heathrow echoing *welcome* all around me. I smiled. I was glad. I suddenly felt like I had come home!

Ahead, I saw the signs for passport control, sighing as I noticed two very long queues; one for British nationals, which I joined and the second for citizens of other nations. The area was vast and well lit. The interior decor was nice and the texture of the carpet was soft, cushioned, smooth and plush. What an absolute dream it was to walk on! I also realised that I finally felt warm.

My queue moved pretty fast and when it was my turn, an elderly looking immigration officer stretched out his hands to take my passport. On checking my passport photograph, he shot a quick glance at me from beneath his varifocals to verify me as the rightful owner. He checked the outer cover and the inside of my British passport, which may have been due to the simple fact that I was coming from Africa.

A shadow of doubt must have crossed the officer's mind, hence it was checked and double-checked to ascertain its authenticity.

Hurrah for me! It was found to be genuine and I skipped past the baggage reclaim area since I had no luggage to collect. My belongings were with me and I was no longer feeling the cold. Happy days!

At the green *nothing to declare* area, there was surprisingly not a single customs officer in sight. I had nothing to declare, but there was no one to stop me even if I had. However, as I walked through, two male officers unexpectedly appeared from nowhere, which startled me. It never occurred to me that most custom officers are *to some extent,* psychologists, trained to watch your every move from behind a screen and from public view.

'Hello Madam', said the taller of the two, sounding very pleasant. 'Can I see your passport please?' He put out his hand and I passed it over to him. He flipped through a few of the pages and then paused to read some of the contents. At one point, he conferred briefly with his colleague for affirmation *(or so I guessed)*, nodded his head and afterwards handed it back to me.

'Is this your only luggage please?' The second officer asked, pointing at my two small bags. 'Did you pack your bags yourself? Did anyone give you anything to carry for them?'

'Yes', I replied, as I gladly handed them over, including my handbag, 'and no, no one has given me anything to carry.' I would never carry any luggage for anyone, having seen what happened to the innocent Nicole Kidman *(who was a mule for a drug smuggler in the 1989 Australian mini-series Bangkok Hilton, based on events in a Bangkok prison).* An eye-opener it was, indeed! Anyone who has watched it and still has the guts to traffic drugs is certainly not from this planet of ours.

My bags were checked. Absolutely positive I had nothing to hide or declare, I thought I had been certified okay. To my surprise, the taller officer handed me a form to read and sign, then pointed at a chair for me to sit on. I was seated and he told me that he had sent for a female officer to search me.

'She will be with you in about two minutes', he said as he smiled, being pleasant again, which was comforting.

I am heterosexual, but I personally think a person of the same sex should conduct a frisk search. I had no problem whatsoever and felt at ease with being frisked by another woman. Briefly, my mind drifted to the opposite kind of scenario, where in a place such as Lagos *(or rather, most parts of Nigeria)*, some men or even a number of male police officers would certainly be more than willing *(if possible)*, to frisk a woman. In the event that it ever happened to me, who would I report the matter to? *The same male police officers?* Hmm. I dreaded the thought!

While waiting for the female officer, I started reading the form that I had been given. It stated they were to search me. I had no problem with that, but I had to find out the reason or reasons why, so I decided to ask the more pleasant and taller of the officers.

'Excuse me Sir, can you kindly explain to me the reasons for this, please?'

'Certainly', he said and thanked me for being very calm, polite and patient and then explained. 'Every traveller is a potential suspect of either having in their possession any type of Class A drugs, or of being a drug trafficker. For this reason, I am afraid to inform you Madam, that although we have nothing against you personally, we are simply carrying out our job. My word of advice to you, however, is that it would be in your best interests to cooperate fully with us in order to get things over with as quickly as possible.'

Satisfied with his explanation, I thanked him and then quickly read the form, signed it and handed it back to him as the female officer arrived.

'Hello Madam, my name is Catherine. How are you doing today?' She said sternly, trying hard to *crack* a smile as she greeted me, but only to reveal a smile as false as her long nails, which disappeared as quickly as it came. Without giving me a chance to reply to her, she immediately grabbed my signed form from the table and browsed through it.

From her body language, I instantly sensed she was standoffish and certainly not as friendly as the tall customs officer was. Fully aware that she was not there to make friends with me, I, on the other hand, thought it would not kill her to loosen up a bit. She was tall, pretty and blonde-haired with a Cockney accent stronger than that of the other two officers put together. 'Do you mind coming with me into a private room for the search?'

'Not at all', I replied.

'So come along please', she said, pointing in the direction of the room. She turned around and I fell in step beside her. Together, we began walking towards the room, which was some 15 metres away.

'Your flight, was it okay?'

'Just fine, thanks', I replied. All the while, thinking to myself that it was only a search. *For Christ's sake, how difficult could it be?*

On entering the room, the officer explained she was going to check my person. Again, I did not object since it was only a routine check and no big deal. Little did I know how wrong I was!

The officer asked me to undress from my waist downwards as she put on a pair of gloves. I obeyed. Shortly after, she asked me to touch my toes, while she inserted something into me to check if I was carrying drugs or anything else *(I had no idea what it was, for I was not forewarned)*. I was mortified and shocked to the core. Never, ever have I been so humiliated in my life and I felt like a common criminal.

To check if I was carrying drugs or doing drug runs, someone had to make me strip almost completely and have me bend forwards to thrust something inside of me? It was agonising and humiliating. No, dehumanising, preposterous and unbelievable were the words. Anyway, I was certified clean!

The officer must have seen the embarrassment written all over my face after the ordeal and I assumed she was accustomed to seeing people's reactions. Without delay, she apologised saying, 'I'm awfully sorry. I know it was pretty uncomfortable but I had to carry out my job.' *Yeah a proper jobsworth, I thought!*

Yet, I said nothing, at least not straight away. How could someone who had just gone through such a distressing experience that was as demeaning as *rape,* find her voice immediately? Shock-horror was an understatement! I felt violated, empty and void of all honour. Silently, I put my clothes back on, but felt like a rape victim trying to gather what was left of the dregs of her womanhood.

With my clothes back on, I felt as though a bit of my dignity had been restored. Thereafter, I informed her that I had something to say and began. 'Catherine, I was of the understanding that you were going to carry out a quick search on me from the waist downwards, which I agreed to. Never did I imagine it would involve any penetration of any kind, let alone some form of poking and probing something inside of me. I'll have you know that I felt and still feel insulted and violated.'

Catherine apologised for the umpteenth time and in her defence, she said, 'I have done nothing out of the ordinary, but only carried out my duty according to section...*blah, blah, blah...' I cannot remember the exact section she quoted.*

She continued, 'I do understand how you feel and I can only apologise for any inconvenience caused. Besides, you did give us your consent by reading and signing the form. Should you wish to make any complaints or take this further, I will give you a card with my details and you can do just that.'

On that note, and with her putting it like that, what were my chances? If she was bold enough to want to give me her details, then she was sure she would have no case to answer and that she would definitely win. According to her, she was simply carrying out her duty. In all honesty, I merely browsed through and did not read the small print on the form I was given to read and sign.

For that reason, I must accept responsibility for the matter. The lesson I learnt is always to read everything properly, whether in normal, small, fine or mouseprint print. Although, the painful truth was, even if I had read the content in small print, had fully understood it all, and later, had refused the search *(being well within my rights),* it would have appeared to them that I had something to hide, which would have meant further delay.

In addition, my being a novice and a complete JJC *(Johnny Just Come – Nigerian slang for a recent arrival or a naive newcomer)* did not help. After all, what did I know anyway? In view of the above, my hands were tied and there was absolutely nothing I could do about it. I simply said it was okay, then Catherine shook my hand, escorted me out of the customs area and said good-bye. I never bothered asking for her details, even though I still felt traumatised. Instead, I *slunk away* in shame *like a lonely rain-soaked kitten in an alleyway,* and walked towards the arrivals lounge.

On my way, I wondered if that was the proper procedure for searching every female visitor arriving into the United Kingdom, contrary to what the male customs officer had said. Even so, the truth of the matter was, correct procedure or not, what could I have done about it? It was such a horrific experience and never before have I mentioned or talked about it to anyone until I wrote this book.

The arrivals lounge was crowded and there were many people looking out for their friends, family or passengers. A few of them were carrying name cards, boards and placards bearing the names of the people they were waiting for. I was not expecting anybody to meet me so I did not bother to look out for anyone or to check any of the name cards.

Gradually, I began to feel more at ease and I was no longer cold. The heated *poking* room had warmed me right through during the half hour or so that my nightmare lasted. I quivered at the thought, although, *I would rather brave a storm than have to go through that a second time.*

In all fairness, Catherine was not as bad as I had initially presumed. She was just doing her job. Determined to put my ordeal with the customs officer behind me, I decided to dust myself off and try the cold again.

I ventured out to locate a taxi rank, but when the automatic doors opened, the force from the strong wind almost threw me backwards. It was like a hurricane as seen on television and it required all of my energy to steady myself and to maintain my balance.

All the while, I kept wondering how I was going to go out there. Then I shifted my bags and myself and stood in a corner for a time, away from the doors. With the few seats in sight fully occupied in the heavily packed out hall, I knew there was no danger of me resting my backside even for a second.

'Now or never', I muttered as I eventually braced myself to confront the cold weather again, and with renewed energy, made my way out of London Heathrow Airport into the streets.

Outside, I realised that wearing my summer clothing was nothing short of suicide. The weather was so bitterly cold, I could not only see my breath, I could also taste it! Oh gosh! How I missed the sunshine and warmth of Nigeria. *Was I already feeling homesick?*

Seeing the long queue of waiting taxis ahead, I walked briskly to the first one in the queue, opened the back door, dashed onto the seat of the Morris Minor and shut the door.

★ ★ ★

'Hello Madam. Where to?' The Taxi *(Black Cab)* driver asked, turning his head to face me as I slouched into the back seat shivering; my teeth chattering from the chill. 'Cold, innit', he said in a Cockney accent, smiling to reveal a set of tobacco-stained teeth that looked more like a burnt down fence, accompanied by a whiff of his breath. Thank God the smell was brief due to the sliding glass screen partition. Perhaps his intercom was faulty.

'Hi', I managed to mumble, placing my bags down next to me and freeing my hands to pass him the blotchy piece of paper containing my Mum's address. The information on the crumpled paper was barely legible due to the coldness of my clammy hands. As a result, I panicked because I thought the driver would not be able to read it. I only nodded my head in reply to his second question.

The driver was a soft-spoken senior citizen, not great to look at, but he resembled one's grandpa with the word *safe* stamped on his forehead to instil confidence in his passengers. To top it off, he was also endowed with a

Kenny Rogers full head of white hair and facial stubble that was long enough to plait.

Just before getting off the plane, I rummaged through my bag for my Mum's address and held it tightly as if my life depended on it. That was before realising that my damp hand would render it almost illegible. Poor old man, I thought to myself, as he struggled to make sense of the content. A few minutes later, he shouted with all the glee of a scientist who had made an important discovery. 'Got it! Stoke Newington.' Speedily, he turned on the ignition, put the car into gear and swung onto the highway, as pleased with himself as if he had just solved a puzzle worth a million pounds.

I thanked him. It was a miracle he was able to read it, even with his spectacles as thick as milk bottle bottoms. I was unable to read it and without the correct address, I was doomed. There would have been no other choice for me but to have headed straight for the homeless centre, since my Mum's contact number was also on the same tatty piece of paper.

Although the driver had done well by being able to read it and deserved a pat on the back, I was beginning to wonder if he would want something more. A tip would be more than likely, I thought, and to discourage any designs of that nature, I began dropping hints that his fare would not be on the high side.

'Visiting for the first time?' Grandpa Stubble *(driver)* asked as he slid open his screen, trying to engage me in a conversation.

'No. Funnily enough', I replied, 'I was born here, but left for Nigeria with my parents when I was five years old. I'm English!' All of a sudden, Grandpa Stubble slammed his foot on the brakes. I thought he was having a heart attack.

'What's your name dear?' he asked, after coming to a complete halt on a kerb, and then regaining his composure. I was petrified because I thought something bad had happened to him. He was speaking, thank God, *but oh no, not the smell again!*

'Irene', I said, still wondering what the matter was, completely terrified.

'Irene. Nice name! Now, please listen', he said, turning to face me. 'You must never, ever, refer to yourself as English again, for you are not!' He continued, 'If you were born here, you are British, but certainly not English. You have just said your parents are from which country again, erm... Nigeria?' he asked, raising an eyebrow. I was too stunned to answer, so I only nodded.

What with the *customs palaver,* it is no wonder I was in shock again for the second time in one day. It seemed I was the one heading for a heart attack. I was gobsmacked, for I never expected this from the *fake safe-looking, Kenny Rogers wannabe and dragon breath grandpa stubble.* Surely, looks can be very deceiving and there was definitely nothing soft about the way he spoke now.

I could not take it anymore but I said nothing, although I was close to tears. By this time, I had made up my mind that London was an awful place and I did not belong here. I got it all wrong at the airport when I thought the walls of Heathrow echoed *welcome,* which made me feel like I had come home.

I was happy too soon, for the echo may well have been *go back.* Anyway, after I had seen my Mum and Gloria, I would go back to Nigeria, I promised myself that much. Grandpa Stubble then turned on the engine and started to drive since I had totally ignored him and his advice.

What's more, I could not figure out which was worse, his bad breath or his advice. I was almost suffocating from his odours. *Holy moly! Was his belly rotten or was it a fart that was making the smell linger? Surely this must be against the law for a taxi, and Stubble should be done for air pollution?*

He probably forgot to slide back his screen or he deliberately wanted to punish me, but either way, I was too scared to ask him to shut it. The weather was too cold to wind down the car window and it would be like adding salt or pepper to an already festering wound.

Through his mirror, he noticed my countenance and apologised, stating that he had never intended to upset his passenger and assured me he was only kidding. *Kidding? Yet it was enough to slam on his brakes, thereby bringing the taxi to such an impromptu halt? Yeah right, if he was joking, then I'm truly a monkey's aunt.*

He then burst out laughing to create a happy atmosphere after he had already polluted it. The man is possessed, I thought, totally something else, and what a shameless old driver turned comedian! *Stick to your driving but try not to take your passengers to hospital in the process.* All the same, I had no choice but to laugh at him rather than with him and I brushed his ambiguous *joke/advice* aside.

I had nothing much against the old man *(just his jokes and his mannerism, which were in itself pure torture),* but I definitely did not like him enough to share any part of his whiff. Really, I preferred him to keep his odours to himself and more seriously, I wanted no more of his stunts, in case his brakes failed him next time.

'How amazing', I whispered softly. My eyes filled with awe at the beautiful scenery as we sped towards the city of London. Grandpa Stubble tried to start another conversation, but I was not interested. He quickly got the message since I only replied when spoken to or answered his questions briefly to discourage him from talking.

Thankfully, he eventually slid back his screen. The heater in the taxi was on full blast, but it actually took a while to thaw my joints as the shock had almost knocked me for six. I rubbed my hands together for extra warmth, while my eyes wandered through the window towards the streets.

I had no idea I was going to be as enthralled by the beautiful scenery as I was while the taxi cruised by. Therefore, I had to shake it all off; thoughts of the cold weather and Grandpa Stubble's *smelly joke advice*, in order to enjoy the sightseeing-like tour. The bright city lights were fascinatingly glittery and brilliant. The Victorian houses were awesome and the skyscrapers, lovely cars, underground entrances, black cabs and the red double-decker London buses were all exciting to see.

There were a number of *bobbies on the beat,* dressed in their smart uniforms and patrolling in pairs. Most of the streets were clean and tidy, with several people walking past, a few were sat down and some, just loitering outside restaurants, wine bars, pubs and clubs. It was astonishing to catch a glimpse of quite a few people with their faces painted in different colours, as well as a group of street punks with pierced faces. Most of them had their hair dyed all sorts of crazy colours, styled in liberty spike Mohawks and were wearing Dr. Marten boots or other unusual footwear.

How intriguing it was to see how busy, bustling and cosmopolitan the streets of London were. Although some were very unfamiliar to me because I left the city a long time ago, I could vaguely remember a few things, such as the red London buses, the wig-like hats of the Queen's guards, black cabs, fish and chips and their distinct aroma, red post-boxes, Dr. Who and the Daleks.

My parents *(Matthew and Jayne)* first came to England with employment vouchers in the 1960s under the Commonwealth Immigration Act 1962, to seek greener pastures. At some point, Mum gave birth to a few of us in London and we all went back to Nigeria in December 1972. I was only five years old when I left England and I merely saw things that bore a semblance to what I was used to associating with London, from the television.

★ ★ ★

The taxi driver pulled up in front of the lovely Victorian house that my Mum and Gloria were renting in Stoke Newington. I paid the fare and thanked him for the sightseeing tour and eventful ride *(which was almost pleasant since he later kept both his mouth and his partition shut).*

As soon as I knocked on the door, Gloria screamed with joy as she saw me through the door viewer. I heard her excitedly shout out to Mum as she rushed to open the door, nearly knocking me over with excitement as she and Mum both tried to hug me at once.

'Oh Gloria, Mum!' I sighed, the three of us almost collapsing in a heap of jackets by the door as I was about to enter the house. 'I have not come all the way from Nigeria just to break a leg you know!' I cautioned jokingly, happy to see them too. They both looked well.

'Cheeky', Mum said, about breaking a leg. 'At least your sense of humour is still intact.'

'I'll never throw it away', I said mockingly, 'I'd rather keep it than give it to Gloria!'

Gloria did not respond verbally. Instead, she smiled and made naughty, comical facial expressions at me. They helped me with my luggage and we made our way into the cosy living room which was lovely and tidy. Almost immediately, I spotted the gas fire and sat on the floor next to it *(stretching my hands towards the fireplace alcove for extra warmth),* almost embracing it. As soon as I sat down, an excited barrage of questions, compliments and greetings were thrown at me. The noise was loud as I also tried to exchange pleasantries with them.

'We've missed you terribly', said Mum.

'Oh, yes!' Gloria added. 'It's so good to see you after such a long time.'

'I've missed both of you too.'

All of a sudden, Mum looked puzzled and asked, 'Why are you alone? The plan was for you to travel with Auntie Ota. Where is she?'

'Oh, I lost her ages ago Mum, however, I will fill you in later.' She was referring to the Auntie who I had travelled with from Nigeria.

I imagined them anxiously waiting to see me, as Mum had not seen me in two years and neither had Gloria, in over a year. I also missed them terribly when they left Nigeria.

'Irene, is this all you wore to come here? Do you want to catch your death of cold? Ah, were you sick during the flight? I know you always suffer from travel sickness. Did you eat on the plane? How was the journey, was it smooth? Was the trip turbulent? Are you alright?' Mum and Gloria were bombarding me again.

'Yeah, yeah and the pilot I never clapped my eyes on was a good-looking bloke too. Haba!' I said, using another Nigerian exclamation while trying to answer all their questions at once.

'Yes, I am alright, except your questions are being fired at me one after the other without any breaks, as if they are going to go out of fashion tomorrow if you do not ask them today. Just calm down for goodness' sake and give me a break. I know you are anxious to get them all out, but please, *chill!*' I said laughing, 'You will both get a chance to ask your questions when I have allocated different time slots for you and your daughter. Right now, I am travel-weary and jet-lagged, so I would like to relax please, if that's okay?' I finished off, smiling and having a fake celebrity moment, although secretly loving the fuss being made of me.

Mum smiled, but shook her head and sucked her teeth, making a hissing sound that could last as long as only she could make it, and it was long; I mean, really long, being the hissing champion that she was. As young kids we had tried, but no one could beat her record. Instead, we would often sit down and watch, secretly timing how long she hissed for at a time.

'Cheeky so-and-so', she later said after hissing for eternity. *Mrs Hissy* then made her way to the kitchen to check on the food cooking on the gas cooker. *Poor woman*, I thought, after telling her off for the thousand-word-per-minute question session, I bet she was not looking forward to asking me about the rest of my siblings at home. That notwithstanding, she did eventually ask later, albeit much more slowly.

'You look so thin, dear!' It was more of a statement from Mum who was now returning into the living room, carrying two mugs of hot Horlicks, one in each hand for Gloria and I.

'Don't worry, Mum, we'll soon fatten her up', Gloria chuckled cheekily as she grabbed her drink and muttered a quick thanks, 'after stuffing her with loads of pounded yam and meat.'

It was my turn to make silly faces at Gloria.

'Are you okay?' Mum asked, giving me the once-over inspection with her eyes, her beautiful face filled with love and concern. I nodded my head in reply to her question and thanked her as she handed my drink to me. I sipped at it, scalding as it was, it tasted so nice.

'Hmm, I needed that', I said. Had she read my mind? Mums always know best, anyway. I proceeded to narrate my ordeal at the hands of the cold and Grandpa Stubble, deliberately leaving out the customs part. I was too ashamed to mention it.

'Mum, Glo, I cannot begin to tell you how much I have suffered today', I said, getting up from the floor. The heat from the alcove was getting unbearably hot and it was making me feel uncomfortable.

'You poor thing! The taxi driver is a mad old fool', Mum said, as she left us again to check on the food she was preparing in the kitchen, only to return a few seconds later.

'You should have told me when he dropped you off and I would have given the ignorant geriatric my piece of advice too', stated Gloria, being the ever-protective sister. 'Anyway forget him, for he is irrelevant'. Gloria added, then exclaimed, *'Nawa o,* so how did you cope, knowing how cold you always were, even in Nigeria? Whatever happened to that famous red hooded jumper of yours?'

Everyone knew about my red hooded jumper because I regularly wore and washed it, again and again, in Nigeria. The jumper was sent to me as a gift from Mum and it was my comforter. In fact, I would have brought it with me, but for my cousin Stella, who wanted to keep it as a souvenir to remember me by *(or so she said, as she snatched it off me).*

As Gloria's heart is forever in the right place, she immediately dashed upstairs to her room to get me her pink fluffy housecoat even before I had the chance to answer her. She noticed I had become cold and had started to shiver again within a few minutes of moving away from the fire. I was glad to have the housecoat, but it was not warm enough for *Miss Cold-blooded*.

'I did not cope, Gloria', I said after thanking her for the housecoat. Savouring the fluffiness, it felt very comforting, soft to touch and smelt of vanilla and rose petals; more like a combination of vanilla and strawberry ice cream flavour.

'Hmm', I said, as the thoughts of yummy ice cream crept into my mind, although, detesting the coldness. 'I'm not sure this will be enough to keep me warm. Sorry, I died a thousand times today in the cold.'

'I can imagine', she said, rolling her eyes as she went upstairs again to get a thick fluffy blanket she called a duvet. I had never seen one before *(well, I don't remember),* but when she came back with it and handed it to me, I felt a lot warmer after covering myself with it.

'That's better.' I said to Gloria. 'Thank you.'

'You're welcome', she said, in a fake British accent, mincing, just to prove she arrived before me and we all laughed at her, while Mum went to the kitchen.

'Ah, Gloria, you naughty girl', I said, telling her off. 'Why did you not write to inform me about how cold it was? Or did you want to purposely punish me?'

'You must be kidding!' Gloria said, looking bemused. 'We are merely in October and summer has only just barely gone. This is not cold yet.'

'Sum...mer? Gloria, you are a joker! I feel as if I am in the Antarctic.'

'There is no such thing as cold or bad weather', Gloria shot back teasingly, 'but only a case of bad or wrong clothing. What did you expect, arriving like this? Wished your destination was the Bahamas, huh?'

'No Hawaii!' I mocked, sucking my teeth briefly, a poor imitation of Mum's gift. One would think I was adopted at birth and not her daughter as I would have inherited her hissing tendencies or perhaps, would have learnt to hiss properly, like her.

'Mum', Gloria called out to Mum in the kitchen, 'be prepared to take your daughter back to Naija *(slang for Nigeria),* before she dies here.' Facing me, she then said, 'Firstly, you know how much I hate writing letters. Secondly, if you did decide to come, I would have thought it would be in the hot summer. In fact, I never believed you would come now until you knocked on the door, *madam!* I was ready to advise our dear Mum to go and get a refund before she lost the money for your ticket.'

'And thirdly?' I said, knowing there was more to come.

'Yes, thirdly', Gloria continued, loving the sound of her own voice, 'it simply did not occur to me that the current weather would be like that of the North Pole to you. Well, the truth is, cold or not, even if I'd known, I could not be bothered doing anything. *Sorry!* Anyway, you are here now. Welcome to England my beautiful sis...ter, nice to see you, to see you, nice! Just as Brucie would say', she finally finished, laughing, giggling and trying to tickle me in order to make me laugh.

'Who the hell is Brucie? You witch. You must have gotten a new broomstick to fly even in the afternoon. *Wickedness girl!'* I said, and we all burst out laughing, including Mum in the kitchen, joining in at the mention of the phrase *wickedness girl*.

The story behind the phrase is about one of the girls we grew up with in Nigeria *(very close to home actually)*. She could not speak English properly so we often laughed and made fun of her. Whenever she cursed, this phrase was all she said and all she ever knew.

Oh, memories! How I missed Nigeria. I was so glad to see both my Mum and sister. Although we had often fought like cat and dog as young children, it was not until now that I realised how much I loved and had missed Gloria.

any contraception. Either that or she may have had a phobia of buying some, which seems a more reasonable explanation. Frankly, had she used any, I dread to think which one of us would have been *deleted.*

Her excuse, each time we teased her about it was the fact that she wanted a male child who never came until the fifth attempt. Nonetheless, whatever her reasons were, we could never have asked for better siblings from our most wonderful Mum, the best of the best!

Mum, truly, is a very down-to-earth, humble, kind and passionate woman. In her younger days, she was a moderate disciplinarian, but even so, she was regularly our pacifist whenever we got into trouble or had to face Dad's wrath, as she often suffered the brunt of it all while protecting us.

As a caring and loving mother, she relentlessly went out of her way to fend for us when things were difficult and she uncompromisingly showed us great affection. I remember how much we loved snuggling up together in her bed most evenings, telling tales, jokes and stories, laughing and generally just being happy. While we were having our happy moments with Mum, Dad often had the habit of pushing the door open on his return from his outings. He would throw us *his look*, as though we were planning a *coup d'état,* shake his head and then leave, rather than join us. Simply Mumtastic our Mum; always there for us!

As the second born and the second female child, I was named Irene at birth. To be honest, I often wondered what my parents were thinking of when they gave me that old name, out of all the names in the world they could have chosen. All the same, taking into account the meaning of Irene *(goodness and peace),* I must confess, without intending to blow my own trumpet, that my parents did not do too badly after all, for I am *supposedly* the gentlest, quietest and most peace-loving member of my family.

I do, however, have my weak points, which include the tendency to be very choosy about the company I keep, I often am a bit too meticulous and I am very fussy with food or normally just finicky about nothing in particular. To top it off, I am quite stuck in my ways and have strong principles.

On the other hand, I am very conscientious, likeable, kind-hearted, sociable and hardworking. Considering these facts with the added benefits of being a Virgo *(the star of perfection),* I never fail to admit that I am far from perfect, although I continually strive to be a perfectionist.

My siblings all had their individual personality characteristics, strengths and weaknesses while growing up and our uniqueness made our household an interesting place to live.

My sister Christine is the eldest. Growing up, she was the sensible and no-nonsense one. Even so, her heart was always in the right place and she cared for us all. Gloria and Michelle (3rd & 4th) were the troublemakers in the family and they could independently start a great war between them.

On a troublesome scale of one to ten, ten being the highest, Gloria would be an eight. She could bring down anyone single-handedly, big or small, but on the contrary, she also has the kindest and the biggest heart in the world. Michelle would be a number five on the scale.

Max, the first male, but 5th child, was very easy-going, Geraldine, also known as Gezza, the 6th born and last girl, was at that time, the eyes and ears of the family. We called her *Gezza the wireless (radio)* because not even a fly could buzz without her noticing it. If anything ever went missing in the house, you could be sure Gezza would be able to find it. Michael, the 7th and last, born much later, was the baby we all doted on.

★ ★ ★

I had a chest murmur at birth, which involved my later having to have daily injections at the UBTH before attending school in the mornings. Dad never compromised my health issues and he did all he could to help me get better, for which I am very grateful. This went on until I was eight years old. My illness did affect my growth and I was slightly smaller than my peers. Fortunately, I was, and I still am being compensated and blessed by God with many good qualities, for this apparent shortcoming. Suffice to say, I am not an ugly duckling but no supermodel either.

When we initially arrived in Nigeria, we had the luxury of house helps *(domestic or servant synonymous with most elite families)* to assist with the domestic duties. Gradually, Dad and Mum made us learn to do the chores as we got older and the number of house helps reduced with time.

My illness never prevented or hindered me from doing anything I set my heart upon and I carried out my chores diligently. Dad noticed! I became his tomboy; the one he could always rely on to do things perfectly. This was to the extent that I was called upon on many occasions to do most of the petty jobs around the house as if I were his only child. After a while, I felt cheated, as it seemed more like punishment to me.

Gloria, *Miss Troublesome,* often took advantage of my cuteness and frequently picked fights with me because she was slightly bigger, but I beat her *(using my seniority as an advantage)* each time she did. Mother dearest regularly made me feel special by reassuring me that the best things in life always come in cute packages. She also teased and referred to me as *the one that beauty prevented from growing taller.* Therefore, in my mind's eye, I was little *Miss Cutelicious!* Mum's wise words constantly made me feel like a princess and they boosted my confidence greatly.

★ ★ ★

Schooling in Nigeria from primary school to the tertiary institution, *for me,* was quite fun. The norm or trend of schooling in Nigeria *(which could be regarded as the right order to follow)* is: First and foremost; to attend kindergarten, nursery or pre-school, then primary school, followed by secondary school. The next big step is to attend a university, polytechnic or other higher institution. Studying beyond this or furthering one's education by gaining other higher qualifications such as a Master's degree or PhD thereafter, is a bonus and a matter of choice or cash.

My siblings and I attended Victory Primary School, off Ewah Road in Benin City. A normal school day starts at 8.00a.m. and ends at anytime between 3.00p.m. and 5.00p.m. The subjects taught, including French and Spanish, are the same as those in schools in England, apart from the added bonus of learning some native Nigerian languages and cultural studies.

During my primary/secondary school days, most of the teachers were very strict and they instilled discipline in us for our benefit because they wanted the best for us, their pupils. In return, most of us often behaved quite well or the punishment would be severe.

Punishment was even harsher if a teacher reported a child to his or her parents, whenever he or she misbehaved. It certainly meant being punished twice, in school as well as at home. For that reason, we always tried to avoid doing things that would necessitate our teachers to report us to our parents, as that could, apart from procuring double punishment, bring shame upon our families.

Corporal punishment in the form of flogging, caning or grass cutting *(to cut grass manually with a cutlass or machete),* were used as forms of punishment by both parents and teachers in Nigeria during my time. It is, however, likely, that these methods may have now been abolished, although they did us no real harm then.

★ ★ ★

As children, we only played or mixed with a handful of our neighbours' kids for a few hours daily. Dad hired a private tutor called Rawson, who arrived at our house on a rickety old bicycle three days a week, to give us extra tuition after school. He was an albino who we nicknamed *(the unfortunate European)*. At first, we loathed him because he derived absolute pleasure in striking our knuckles with the edge of a ruler each time we got his questions wrong. To us, it was pure wickedness, and believe you me, he suddenly stopped doing that after we taught him a lesson or two.

Each time he arrived at our house, he would religiously lock up and chain his bicycle to a fence. Mysteriously, the keys to his bicycle went missing a couple of times when it rained heavily and he had no choice but to walk home in the downpour.

After a while, we bravely confronted him about his method of discipline and we came to a compromise which worked well in our favour *(the knuckle hitting stopped and his keys no longer vanished)*, until Dad found out.

I would say we preferred *the unfortunate European's* punishment to Dad's of a hundred *pick pins* each *(a punishment where one crouches down on one leg to touch the ground with one finger and maintains that same position for a long time, during which one perspires profusely and writhes in pain that spreads to all parts of the body, amid messy mucous streaming from the nostrils)*. The worst part of it was not being allowed to stop, even for a second, to wipe one's nose.

★ ★ ★

By the time I was nine years old, we only had one house help left and she was a distant relative called Isoken. As a result, we had no choice but to do most of the chores ourselves. I vividly remember the day Mum asked me to slaughter a chicken so she could prepare some chicken stew for our dinner. We had a poultry coop filled with agricultural fowls *(well-developed chickens that we reared and fed with synthetic feed)* and I could take my pick.

Christine was away at the boarding school for her secondary education and Isoken had gone to the market to buy *only God knows what.* Therefore, I was next in line and the only one available to carry out the gruesome task of slaughtering a chicken. *'Me, slay a chicken?'* I thought to myself. *'When I cannot even kill a fly!'* I was terrified.

I panicked as I made my way to the poultry coop at the back of the house to grab hold of one of the chickens. After what seemed like a two-hour struggle trying to catch just one of them, I eventually succeeded.

Sadly, it seemed the poor chicken had already guessed the fate that was about to befall it and it started flapping its wings furiously. I was nervous too, but I gripped it tightly and then took it a few metres away from the other chickens for the slaughter. I got a knife, placed the chicken on the floor and held it down with both of my legs pressed against each wing to hold it down firmly. *I had seen people doing this regularly, halal style.* It was normal and happened every day in Nigeria, but was something I had never, ever attempted to do myself until then.

Still holding the chicken down, I was very scared and nervous. No doubt, the chicken must have sensed my fear too, and as I tried to grab its neck, it struck my left hand with its beak. This startled me that I flinched a little, out of panic. In the process, I loosened my grip on the chicken and the silly animal seized the excellent opportunity to escape. It was never found again.

That was the first and last time I ever attempted to kill a chicken! Fortunately, we had plenty of them, which meant losing one hardly mattered much to us, and luckily for me, no one found out. When Isoken returned from the market a few minutes later, I told a little white lie, that Mum had instructed her to slay one of the chickens for dinner. Carrying out Mum's order, she *bumped* one off in no time. To me, she was a *pro!*

★ ★ ★

After completing my primary education in 1979, I sat the Common Entrance Examination and undertook interviews in the same year. I was successful, and gained admission to Idia College, Benin City; one of the best secondary schools in Nigeria at the time. My happiness knew no bounds as I never expected to get into the school due to the tough competition and high standards required of the prospective entrants.

Despite my joy, I really was not looking forward to going to the school since it meant spending five years *(except during school holidays)* away from my family at a boarding school for girls. Fortunately for me, the start date was not until September which I was very glad about.

My parents were very proud of the fact that I was going to become a student at one of the best colleges in the country and told all their friends and our family about it *(if only they knew about the chicken story)*. It was as though I was going to Cambridge or Oxford and I felt on top of the world.

The principal of Idia College, Miss Ruth E.B. Howard, was a shrewd Scottish woman with a remarkable reputation. Every parent wanted their daughter to attend the school, although not everyone was fortunate enough or had the privilege to. Hence, Mum gladly spared no expense whilst purchasing my uniforms from the school tailor. She also bought all the items I needed as listed in the school prospectus and together we arranged my new belongings neatly in my brand-new red and black tartan suitcase. I was excited and ready to begin the big girl's school, but when the time eventually came for me to leave home on a Sunday evening, I cried all the way there. Being a home girl, I hated leaving my family and home.

Upon my arrival, I was assigned to one of the dormitories; the Yellow House, which was also known as *Omu House*. I was shown my top bunk bed and introduced to the senior girl on the bottom bed. After the pleasantries, she promised my Mum that she would look after me.

I made some friends and adapted to living harmoniously with my fellow sister-students. Little by little, I learnt many invaluable lessons as a student, such as good manners, the virtues of cleanliness, discipline and following a routine with attention to detail, etc., all of which has helped me a great deal to date.

In my first year, I learnt the Idia College 'Motto Song', which is as follows:

"Don't you know us, don't you know us, we are Idia girls. If you want to know us, you must learn our motto, hmm, hmm. Honesty, determination and initiative, is our motto."

The name Idia came from the first Queen Mother of Benin. She was the mother of Esigie, the Oba *(King)* of the Benin Kingdom who ruled from 1504 to 1550. She was a strong warrior who played a significant role in the rise and reign of her son as the Oba.

We were cherry picked after the successful completion of our interviews and the selection process, and then later groomed and trained to be only the best. Taking the name of our school into consideration, we acted like little women, then little Queens. We had the airs and graces of royalty, and Queens, we were!

Miss Howard was a strong and brave woman who we aimed to emulate. I am very fortunate to have attended Idia College, for it helped me to become what I am today and I thank my precious Mum for making it possible.

★ ★ ★

Being a dear friend is about being sincere, reliable and trustworthy, which are the amazing qualities I have found to date in my dearest friend Ebitimi Ikwuazom (née Torubiri). The best of friends since childhood, our parents were also good friends, until her dad sadly passed away during our first year at Idia College. We were very close and I am glad that I was there to support and comfort her at the time. Timi *(as I normally call her)* was a very smart, witty and worldly girl, who took no rubbish from anybody.

Growing up, she knew what she wanted and exactly how to get it! She also possesses the biggest and kindest heart, just like my sister Gloria. I was at the boarding school, while Timi was a day student.

The school meals were not always tasty, and because I was very fussy with food, eating posed a big problem. I had to rely almost totally on the provisions I had brought from home, which often ran out very quickly due to my more or less total dependence on them. Aware of how fussy and choosy I was with my food, Timi often brought me food from her home most mornings.

Whenever the refectory lunch menu was eba *(made from garri – a major staple food in West Africa made from cassava tubers)* and soup, which I genuinely disliked, Timi often, bailed me out. She was so generous and kind hearted to the extent that she would rather forgo her transport fare for returning home or her last cash, for me to buy food. Timi would then borrow money for her taxi fare home from one of our fellow students, to be paid back the next day. If unsuccessful, she would walk home instead.

This was typical of Timi, my best friend and sister, although, I regularly returned the favour by taking notes for her each time she missed a lecture. Fortunately, I enjoyed explaining the notes I had taken, and doing so helped me to learn more too.

★ ★ ★

Our daily school routine entailed our getting up at 6.00a.m. to take a shower. After we were dressed, we proceeded to the refectory for breakfast, and then a bell rang to notify us to attend the morning assembly. Following that, we made a 5-minute walk to our classrooms for the marking of the attendance register, followed by lectures, a break and more lectures. The school day ended around 3.30p.m. and the girls in the boarding school *(called boarders)* would return to their dormitories or hostels, while the day students went back to their respective homes to return the next school day.

Lunch was usually after-school hours and we observed a siesta *(or did manual labour on some Wednesdays)*, for one hour. More often than not, we had some free time afterwards to mingle, then went to the refectory again for dinner.

With our full bellies, we would then head back to the classrooms for evening studies, to return to the dorms for bedtime just before lights out. Saturday was inspection day and we cleaned our different dormitories until they were thoroughly spotless. On Sundays, we attended church services on our school premises, but worshiped at a nearby church on special occasions for baptisms, confirmations, and the Christmas Carol service or nativity plays.

Apart from the main public holidays in Nigeria, we also had other holidays, such as Labour Day for Workers, Nigerian Independence Day *(Nigeria gained independence from the United Kingdom on the first day of October 1960)*, Children's National Day *(May 27th)*, Mother's Day and Muslim Celebrations *(Id-El-Fitri, Id-El-Kabir, Id-El-Maulud and Hajire)*.

Children's National Day is regularly observed and celebrated by parents, teachers and children throughout Nigeria. It normally involves a national prayer for every child and a march-past parade session by children in various stadiums and in different cities across Nigeria. We were allowed to visit home briefly after leaving the stadium, to return back to the boarding house at 7.00 pm prompt on the same day.

Our outing day was once a month and it never came quickly enough for me. I always looked forward to visiting my family *(for a few hours)* in my clean pink and purple uniform with matching beret, immaculate white socks and polished brown Cortina shoes from Bata *(one of the largest shoe manufacturers in Nigeria at the time).*

Being at one of the best colleges and at the boarding school gave me a sense of pride. Therefore, I was full of airs and graces and walked with a certain kind of swagger in my uniform during these outings.

★ ★ ★

A number of activities were frequently held during the school terms on different occasions, and I often took part in our yearly inter-house sports festivals by playing volleyball. The competitions took place in our school compound, with students from the various dormitories competing among themselves in a variety of sports.

I was a member of the school choir and of the Lepra Society (formerly The British leprosy Relief Association, now LEPRA Health in Action), *a health and development organisation working to restore health, hope and dignity to people affected by leprosy.* Leprosy is an infectious disease caused by bacteria *(a tiny rod-like germ called mycobacterium leprae),* which affects the skin and nerves. First described by Dr. G.A. Hansen in 1873, it is also known as Hansen's disease (HD).

As a member of the choir, I derived great pleasure in mastering the lyrics of different songs during competitions and I loved dazzling the audiences with my *okay* voice. Fully confident and aware of my assets and

God-given talents, I never failed to use them to my full advantage, bearing my full set of 52 teeth; molars and premolars included *(while everyone else has a maximum of 32).*

My big *blessed gob* was often stretched wide open to its limits, intending to receive captivating smiles and to win the hearts of my audiences. By so doing, I was regularly, but unexpectedly thrust to the forefront a number of times, which often helped us win many competitions.

Miss Howard was a philanthropist to the core and she was all about helping the survivors of leprosy. Before treatment was available, a diagnosis of leprosy meant suffering in pain, being labelled as having an incurable disease and isolated in 'leper colonies'. The sufferers were constantly shunned by society and treated as social outcasts; thus leading to rejection, discrimination, depression and self-worthlessness. Today, antibiotics and a good skin care regime can help to prevent the disease from destroying the body.

There are a number of specialist hospitals for the disease sufferers throughout Nigeria. Upon successful treatment, alternative arrangements are made available for them to be relocated to their new allocated dwelling places, although these are in very remote areas. These far-flung and isolated places *(referred to as settlement villages),* are where the ex-sufferers are expected to rehabilitate and settle with their children, despite being cured of the disease.

We travelled as young Lepra members to Ossiomo Leper Settlement in Edo State to support those who had been segregated from their families or had been banished from their homes. Each time we visited them, we happily helped with their washing and shopping. We often plaited the women and children's hair and encouraged them to participate in various activities such as playing card games, singing and dancing. Our visits gave them hope, encouraged big smiles on their long-suffering faces, gave them a sense of self-worth and made them very happy. These good deeds were extremely rewarding for me, as they in turn, made me feel truly fulfilled.

★ ★ ★

Whenever I was at home during the school holidays, I resumed my role as Dad's tomboy and still the little errand girl. At some point, Dad installed an electronic bell to summon us instead of shouting whenever he needed us. One ring of the bell meant a call for Christine the eldest, two rings for me, three for Gloria and four, five and six times etc., for the rest of my siblings.

We normally gave up listening after three or four rings since it was easy to lose count afterwards. Also, it must have been hard work for Dad buzzing the longer numbers, which we never bothered listening out for. There were times when I actually thought the bell was constantly stuck on two rings as that was the most frequent number of times he pressed the bell. *For me, and I could sometimes hear it in my dreams.*

The only time I had a bit of a breather was whenever the electricity was down. Even then, he would call or shout out, but I often pretended not to hear him. Funnily enough, thinking about it now, I wonder what really happened to that bell after all. Knowing our lot, it would not be surprising if someone had disconnected or destroyed it! *Any guesses as to who that someone might be? Hmm!*

To me, it always seemed like it was my natural responsibility or formal duty to take Dad's briefcase to his car before he went to work each morning. I had to get the same briefcase out of his car and carry it into the house every time he returned home from work *(I often wondered whose job it was while I was away at school)*. If I was not available to do it, he would immediately realise I was out. This was difficult for me growing up, because most of my siblings often got away with more pranks and teenage adventures than I ever did.

One late evening, Dad returned home from one of his outings and asked me to unload the stuff from his car boot. Obediently, I took his bunch of keys and opened the boot, only to find a bucket full of water with about a dozen live, slimy and slippery black catfish swimming in it.

I got very panicky, for I have a phobia of touching or being in such close proximity to any creature other than humans. Therefore, I immediately called out to my sisters for help, but none of them came to my aid, so I braced myself for the task before me. After all, I thought, they were inside the bucket, what harm could they do? *Swim out and then bite me?*

As I reached into the boot to lift out the bucket, my legs began to shake. After a little while, I successfully managed to remove the bucket from the boot and placed it on the floor, heaving a huge sigh of relief. That done, I realised I still had to carry it into the house and all the way to the kitchen, which to me was a Herculean task.

Not only was I deeply terrified at just the sight of the swimming fish, the thought of Dad wondering why I was taking so long to do the task and seeing me in such a lily-livered state, added to my misery. So, I quickly mustered up some courage, grabbed the handle of the bucket and carried it in slowly. My legs were so wobbly that they felt like jelly. It also seemed like I was walking in slow motion.

Still in panic mode, I concentrated solely on the fish; squinting, while thinking that if they dared to swim out of the bucket, it would be *fry* day for them. I continued to hold tightly on to the handle with both hands as though my life depended on it.

The kitchen seemed so far away and it felt like I was taking one step per hour. My sisters sensed my fear and hid in a corner watching and giggling as they knew I was a spineless wimp where insects or animals were concerned.

All of a sudden, something went wrong. I was sprawled across the floor, soaked in a pool of water with a dozen cold, slimy, slippery black catfish swimming and flapping their fins against my skin. What I hated and dreaded the most had happened. *My worst nightmare!*

To date, I cannot remember exactly what happened or how I hit the ground. I must have bumped into something or tripped up and fallen over due to nervousness or because my eyes were fixated on the fish, rather than on where I was going. I must have fainted. I felt like I was in a dazed stupor and all I could hear were sounds of laughter floating by from afar as I lay flat on my back.

Chapter Three:
Turning Point

The year 1980 was a turning point for my family. Dad married a second wife who we nicknamed Steppy and our lives changed forever. Polygamy is a common phenomenon in Nigeria. Any man of means is a sure target for the roving eyes of women who long for a ready-made man and home. Mum was heartbroken and devastated, having laboured tirelessly in the United Kingdom with my dad whilst he studied.

What used to be a peaceful home became a divided one due to the constant fighting and quarrelling, typical of such dysfunctional homes. Dad's attention, love and affection for us became divided. Although, these were not great at any point, it was always just one man, one wife and us, their children; a monogamous family. We had never had to share him with a new bunch of people, as was the case now. Steppy moved in with her sister *(well, that was what she called the spare girl she brought along with her into the marriage)*.

Two wives under one roof was a disastrous idea. We became a polygamous family and gained a lifestyle with which we were not familiar, but that we had to learn fast, regardless. My parents already had six children between them, then Dad got a lot busier and within the space of six years, Steppy gave birth to four boys.

Mum also *snuck* one in around the same time as Steppy's second child. *'She became very broody'*, she said. Mum gave birth to Michael, her youngest and last child, meaning Dad's entire children were eleven in all. *Government the sharp shooter, I bet none of his swimmers got away.*

The eleven of us could easily have formed a club called GUFT, which stands for *Government Un-united Football Team*. Eleven on the field, but I would say 14 is a better number; Dad, Mum and Steppy included as reserves *(not bad and just right for a family of 14!)*

Steppy had no respect or regard whatsoever for my Mum, something that never went down well with us. She must have been a glutton for punishment or just dim-witted, since she was fully aware that she had us to contend with. Revenge is a dish best served cold and nothing gave us greater pleasure when she received her *just desserts* for disrespecting our Mum.

As I was already at the boarding school, I was very glad to be away from most of it all. However, each time I went back to school after the holiday, I not only missed them, but also felt sorry for Mum and my other siblings who experienced the day-to-day turmoil and upheavals that are the signature of a polygamous home.

Whenever I was home on holiday, my siblings and I would assemble *(as usual)* in Mum's safe haven; her bedroom. On one of these occasions as we gathered, chatting and discussing stuff with the door closed firmly behind us, I pointed out that I was concerned about the noticeable change in Dad's behaviour. I also mentioned how unhappy I was about the hostile atmosphere and the entire situation at home due to the constant quarrels.

At that precise moment, I was totally oblivious of the fact that Steppy had her big ears *(which stuck out like the two doors of a Volkswagen Beetle left ajar)* glued to the closed door, eavesdropping. On Dad's return, Steppy recited all I had said to him and he summoned every one of us to his private living room.

Still, I was none the wiser. He then called me out to stand in the middle of the room, blurted out my terrible *blunder* and flogged me extremely hard in front of everyone. I was used as a scapegoat. The purpose of this was to teach us a lesson in not badmouthing his second wife or him. I thought I was going to faint or die that day and I do not know how I managed to survive that flogging. I ached from the pain for weeks afterwards.

The next day, after dad had gone to work, Steppy sat on a chair relaxing and enjoying the cool morning breeze outside. Just as she was about to doze off, Gloria tapped her right shoulder and said, 'We know you were Dad's informant yesterday!' As she was about to deny it, we all surrounded her and Gloria dragged her down from the chair she was sitting on, while we all pounced on her, cursing, kicking and screaming.

After begging for mercy, she knew better than to report her ordeal at our hands to Dad when he returned from work. Nevertheless, after a short while, she soon forgot and resumed her usual whisperings in Dad's ear. All the same, we were pleased that we'd had the opportunity to hit back at her.

Due to all the *aggro* at home, I only went there during school holidays. What a relief! I did not have to engage in all the bickering or watch the injustice being meted out to my darling Mother. On the other hand, going home became a time to catch up on all that had transpired in my absence and as always, I was all ears!

Sadly, what used to be our loving home just became a house.

★ ★ ★

As a teenager, I vaguely remember having crushes on different boys at one time or another, except none of them resulted in anything serious. One though, did linger a little longer than a crush ordinarily should, but I dumped that particular boy as soon as I found out that he was up to no good with other girls.

On hearing the song *Baby Be Mine* by Michael Jackson on the radio and then watching him on the television, I was instantly smitten with both the song and the singer, Michael. I purchased a copy of his *Off the Wall* album, learnt all the lyrics by heart and fell head over heels in love with him. I answered his plea to *baby be mine,* I was his; his greatest fan, and I adored everything about him. In the end, I saved myself for him *only,* the King of Pop, and I dreamt *(just like a billion other teenagers)* of marrying him someday.

★ ★ ★

I completed my secondary schooling, and for my tertiary education, I secured a place at Auchi Polytechnic, which was also in Edo State. I had planned to study Office Management for my Ordinary National Diploma (OND), but unfortunately for me, after I gained my place, I could not enrol for studies because my course of choice was unaccredited.

Waiting for my course to be accredited was like trying to catch a mirage. Even so, I was not unnecessarily bothered or worried. Somehow, I thought the accreditation problem would be sorted out in no time, but I was wrong! I did not discover until it was too late that the accreditation might take an eternity to be put in place.

At some point, I began to grow apprehensive and gradually my fears turned into nightmares as I was still hoping against hope, but the days were rolling into months. I tried to cling on to my optimistic thoughts in a corner of my mind that somehow, at the last minute, a miracle that could save the day would come through for me.

I had never wanted to study any other course apart from Office Management *(a good secretary could earn up to six pounds per hour in England, I was reliably informed)*. As this situation continued, I kept myself busy by studying and attending extra-mural lectures to avoid being idle at home, until the good news finally arrived... Two whole years later!

Two years flew by, just like that! Had I known it would take that long, now with the benefit of hindsight, I would have travelled abroad to be with Mum. Not only had I wasted two whole years waiting, I had to go through the entire process of interviews again, when my admission was supposed to have been guaranteed the first time. Typical! That could only happen to me.

★ ★ ★

Being a student at a higher institution and living on campus with my three roommates, I became independent. Growing up, our parents wanted the best for us and they did all they could to protect us. However, no matter how protected we were, we certainly were not kept under lock and key, neither were we allowed to go out unnecessarily. If it was necessary or extremely important for us to go somewhere, we had to go quickly and to get home before Dad got back, or else...

On campus, I was free as a bird, liberated to do as I pleased and could go anywhere I chose *(free of the Government's shackles and restrictions)*. That notwithstanding, there were limits and boundaries I could not cross. The truth was, deep down, I had been so grounded in the moral values instilled in me by my parents, that I was strong enough to keep myself on the right path, even in their absence.

The virtues of being a disciplined girl and the need to be one at all times and in all places, had been strongly drummed into me. This was to such a great extent that, even when I was thinking about overstepping the boundaries of the moral laws handed down to me, an alarm would simply go off internally, and I would have no choice but to restrain or censure myself.

Whenever I attended parties at night, I was definitely not comfortable after midnight and always found my way back to the campus. I never felt right or safe being out that late, especially in the company of the opposite sex.

I became a member of the Rotary Club *(a group of people organised as a union to promote world peace)* and I loved attending the meetings.

In my second year, I lost the urge and need to continue living on campus. After searching thoroughly for suitable accommodation, I rented a small but cosy room in a building off campus among other students. It was located within walking distance of our Polytechnic.

While relaxing in my room after lectures one sunny afternoon, a few of my friends who were also my course mates paid me a visit. As we were chatting, one of the guys brought out a packet of cigarettes and handed a stick to each of us. I took the cigarette that had been handed to me, held it in my left hand for a while and discreetly tried to watch the others. Without any qualms, they lit their cigarettes and began puffing away.

When one of them noticed I had not lit mine and was not smoking, he threw a lighter to me, which I could not even catch. It fell on the floor and I timidly picked it up. Not wanting to be the odd one out, as I wanted their perception of me to be that of a *modern chick,* I stuck the cigarette between my lips and with trembling hands, lit it. To my amazement, all eyes were on me and everyone in the room started laughing.

Apparently, I had missed the joke and when I asked what appeared to be so funny or amusing to them, they all pointed at me, laughing. Still reeling with laughter, they said I was the butt of their joke *(the cigarette butt of it)*. Yet, I did not understand until one of the girls walked up to me and snatched the cigarette from my lips. I had lit the wrong end!

I felt very foolish and embarrassed. I had wanted to prove to my peers that I had smoked before; that I was no novice, but rather a streetwise and sophisticated girl. Dear me! It was an absolute blunder and I had ended up ridiculing myself. As a result, I felt a lot worse than a novice did; exactly what I never intended them to think I was.

Never before had I touched a cigarette in my life, let alone actually put one in my mouth and lit it. I was unaware that the two ends of a cigarette are for different purposes. As far as I was concerned, the two sides were the same.

Still beside themselves with laughter, I was determined not to be fazed by their ridicule. Therefore, with little trepidation and without knowing exactly where the courage was coming from, I simply picked up from the floor, what was left of my pride. Afterwards, I chased them all out of my room and slammed the door in their faces. Some friends they were, *not!*

Word got round fast. I made headline news on campus! Meanwhile, I lived off campus and boycotted lectures for two days under the pretext of being ill. When I'd had my fill of hiding, a few of my *good* friends urged me not to be ashamed since I had done nothing wrong. They praised me by stating it was decent of me never to have smoked or *roasted* my lungs with cigarettes and I thanked them for their support.

Foolish me, subjecting myself to all that palaver, just to prove some point of such gross irrelevance! A simple *no thanks* or plainly refusing to accept the cigarette would have done the trick. To this day, I have never smoked a cigarette. Smoking is a bad habit I can and will gladly live without. I still believe peer pressure is truly evil, even to this day.

Chapter Four:
What Etiquette?

Joining my Mum and sister in London was very exciting and it reminded me of when I returned home from college. I anxiously wanted Gloria and I to exchange more stories, and to get down to the nitty-gritty of events and news from Nigeria and London. I had plenty of news to share about the happenings from back home in Nigeria and I presumed Gloria had tons of information to share about life in London.

While Gloria and I were busy catching up on old times, Mum brought in a tray carrying the long-awaited food she had finally finished preparing. The tray contained two huge platefuls of jollof rice *crowned* with chicken and fried ripe plantains called *dodo* in Nigeria, a glass of orange juice for Gloria and a can of orange drink *(sweating coldness)* for me. I gobbled up the food without taking a break, then gulped down the drink in one go. Since I was no longer cold, it went down well. Fed and watered, I let out a burp and smiled satisfactorily.

It was so hilarious! Seeing the way I devoured the meal, anyone would assume that I had been starving for weeks, fasting for 40 days, was an F.O.B. *(Fresh Off the Boat, as my friends would jokingly say),* or I had just arrived from one of the most poverty-stricken countries in the world. The food tasted so delicious that it made me realise how much I had missed Mum's mouth-watering meals. I belched again, louder this time.

'Bush girl', Gloria teased. 'Welcome to London again', she said, laughing because, to her, I had thrown decorum, decency and all table manners out of the window.

'Silly Londoner, I don't care', I teased her back, also laughing. There was no need for any etiquette whatsoever. I was home with my family and it was simply like the old days in Nigeria. Oh, how I love my sister!

Chapter Five:
James

Gloria showed me around the cosy, but decent sized two bedroom house after eating and informed me that I was to share her room with her. That was fine by me, as I did not fancy being in a room all by myself, at least, not that soon, anyway. After the tour, we headed for Gloria's beautiful room, now ours, and we sat down on the huge double bed to chat some more.

Thereafter, she began showing me her lovely collection of clothes, taking each item one by one out of the wardrobe, removing them from their hangers and laying them neatly on the bed so I could assess them properly.

'Isn't this lovely, my darling sister?' She asked with a hint of pride, of a particular gown with a floral design and a pinkish hue. She was staring at me and then straightened the creases on it after spreading it out on the bed.

My eyes lit up on seeing her beautiful collection, however, I was not too keen on the one in question, for I am not really into floral prints. Plain and elegant is more my style, although I love the colour pink.

Even if it was a little awkward, I thought I had better agree with her supposition or she would be unhappy. 'Oh yeah, sister dearest, it is cute, well cut.' *I did not like it, but did not hate it either; it was just okay, although not something I would buy myself.*

'You can wear it any time I'm not wearing it', she offered, 'to the shops, outings or for a picnic, anywhere.'

'Oh, that's kind of you. How much was it, if you don't mind me asking please?'

'Take a guess.'

'Hmm', I pondered, trying to come up with how much the dress could be worth. What did I know about pounds and pence anyway? Yet, I decided to give it a go.

'Now, let's talk money, honey.' I said, rubbing the palms of my hands together. 'I would say, ten pounds?' I said in a small voice. I did not want her to be angry, just in case it did cost more than that.

'That's a fortune. I'll give you another chance.'

'Good, that's just what I like about you. Six pounds, then?'

'A pound! Yes I bought it for £1, from 'C & A' during the summer sales.' Gloria said, feeling so ecstatic about her bargain.

'Wow! That's a steal, you know', I replied, scooping the dress up from the bed and admiring it genuinely this time. 'Can I wear it sometime, but at home please?' I pulled my face funnily, now taking into account its cheap and cheerful price.

'Yes', Gloria said. At that point, I gave her a big hug, thanking her with great happiness.

'Oh, it's a pleasure. I will wear this blue suit to church on Sunday. Hang on, I'll show you.' With that, she reached into the floor-to-ceiling, wall-to-wall wardrobe and pulled out a chic and trendy sky blue lady's suit.

I paused slightly, looking at it very critically. 'No, you cannot wear this to church.' I finally managed to blurt out.

'Why not?' Gloria asked, looking puzzled.

'You are tall and leggy and the skirt is short, Gloria. It will reveal too much and won't portray you as the decent girl our parents brought us up to become.'

She then snatched the suit in question from out of my hands, saying, 'This is London, not some church in Nigeria.'

'And Mum allows you to wear this?'

'I said, this is London', she said emphatically and rolled her eyes knowingly.

'Are you angry with me for saying that? If so, I apologise, for I am very sorry. I thought I could express my feelings to you.'

'It's okay. Never mind, your advice is noted.' I knew my advice, if anything, was far from noted, by the way Gloria was suddenly cramming the clothes back into the wardrobe, rather than hanging them neatly on the hangers before putting them away. I bet she was tempted to say, 'Enough, Miss Critical Spirit. *Scram.*'

The relationship became rather frosty, but after a few minutes of talking softly to each other, we put the scene behind us and continued chatting excitedly again as if we hadn't had the minor squabble. I told her about my boyfriend James, back in Nigeria.

'You will love him, Gloria', I said to her, 'he is so charming.' My mind drifted back to James and there was a sudden lump in my throat. My eyes started to well up due to sadness at having left my love, James, behind. Seconds later, I could feel the sting of tears, which soon began to cloud my eyes.

'Oh, please don't cry', Gloria started to comfort me. 'If you love him that much, he can join you here after a while.'

'Is that really possible?' I smiled through the tears, as my face lit up with hope, and Gloria nodded her head in affirmation.

'Won't Mum kill me?' I asked Gloria.

'Nah she won't, Mum's cool!' She said speaking with a fake Yankee accent this time. Gloria sure does learn fast, I thought. She is without doubt a good copycat.

★ ★ ★

I met James in 1988. I was 21 and in my second year, while we were both undergraduates at Auchi Polytechnic. James, a dark and handsome young man was slender, but muscular, with a solid athletic build.

As a sprinter, he took part in various relay and 100-metre hurdle competitions, sprinted his way into my life and then stole my heart with his cool mien and composure. He had a soft, round face with a hint of innocence and a cheeky persuasive smile that could make you do things you never intended to. James, a year older than I am, lived with his parents in Lagos but hails from the Uzzeba region of Owan Local Council, Edo State, Nigeria.

A couple of weeks after I met him, I narrated the cigarette incident to him in order to soften the effect it might have if he heard it from someone else. To my relief, he dismissed it and assured me that I was a good and responsible girl for not smoking in the first place. As a sportsperson, he never smoked or drank too. I was glad.

James and I soon became very close. We did most things together such as eating, bathing, studying, and before long, we realised we were head over heels in love with each other. Moments spent together seemed so special as we would giggle and whisper words affirming our love for one another:

'I love you more than words can ever say, honey', we would chant to each other. I would gaze lovingly into his gorgeous brown eyes and he, into mine.

What I loved most about him was the fact that he was a God-fearing lad. He was very loyal, kind and he adored me. He spent most of his time with me after lectures and even though we both had our separate accommodation off campus and studied different courses, we were almost inseparable.

James was not only a talented sportsman, he was very good at art and he was a karate black belter too. He studied Art & Design, while I studied Office Management. We were young, carefree and penniless, but very much in love, hence escaping to the place I called home off-campus with him was always a better option. A pleasant relief from the constant quarrels at my Father's house!

Time flew by and suddenly, it was time for me to renew my British passport as I had overstayed in Nigeria by 17 years. It meant I had to travel to renew it at the British Embassy in Lagos, the former capital of Nigeria. The plan was for me to join Mum and Gloria in England after my exams, accompanied by one of my aunties, called Ota. I was happy and looking forward to travelling abroad to meet my Mum and sister, but on the other hand, I was sad because that meant leaving James and the rest of my family behind in Nigeria.

Since our relationship was still very young, I had my reservations. Although my close friends knew about it, I purposely kept my plan from James because I wanted him to love me for me and not for my British citizenship. So, in being conservative with the truth, I informed him that I was travelling to Benin City to visit my family. I had no problem with my conscience about this because I was truly going home and also travelling to Lagos with some of my siblings.

I returned to Auchi after I had successfully renewed my passport and at the end of the semester we both travelled to Benin, after which I got off the taxi and his journey continued, to Lagos. It broke my heart each time we parted and I was always in tears, but I eagerly looked forward to seeing him again when we resumed school after the holidays.

The following year, everything was great, my love for James grew stronger and I was certain James was the man I was going to marry. When it was time for my final exams, I studied extremely hard in order to pass with good grades. After my exams, I had to tell him about my plans and dreaded the thought of leaving him behind. Full of guilt, I was devastated and heartbroken beyond imagination. I almost choked on my words when I informed him of my intentions, but he surprisingly took it in his stride and with philosophical calmness.

We then travelled together from Auchi to Benin and parted ways as usual, after I reassured him that I would travel through Lagos to London, and promised, while doing so, to stop by to visit him. That was also to afford me the opportunity to meet my future in-laws.

Chapter Six:
Hasta La Vista, Darlings

In the period between our parting and when I was to travel to London, my heart ached for James. I longed for him daily and missed him terribly. He was only able to telephone me a couple of times from Lagos due to the cost, which was rather expensive. The fact that my dad was very strict, did not help when it came to receiving his calls too. My only consolation was that I would see him on my way to London.

Mum sent my plane ticket a week before my departure, which confirmed the date and my travel details to London. Full of joy and excitement, I informed most of my friends and family members of my trip. They were happy for me, but also sad because they were going to miss me. However, they did not hesitate to take possession of almost all of my belongings, on the assumption that I would be able to acquire a lot more, and better ones abroad.

The day of my departure arrived and I bade my sisters and brothers whom I love dearly, farewell. I was going to miss them a lot and it broke my heart as we all cried together. I prayed for God to take good care of them, especially since Mum was not there. While Dad took me to Auntie Ota's house, I appealed to him to be soft on my siblings. I was very sad and cried all the way there.

Remembering that day still brings fresh tears to my eyes; even while writing this now after almost 23 years. I am not one for farewells. I really hate goodbyes and I try to avoid doing them if possible.

On the way, Dad *dished out* some fatherly advice that made me feel even more emotional, and on reaching my Aunt's house, I tried very hard to compose myself by trying to act brave. She was ready when we got there and after I had helped her put her luggage into the boot of the car, Dad drove us to the domestic airport in Benin.

I could feel the tears welling up in my eyes again as we reached the airport. I said goodbye to my Dad and when I gave him a hug, I noticed that his eyes were brimming with tears too, but he quickly wiped them away. My heart sank, as I had never seen that before *(not even when his Dad died. I must really be special)*. I never knew he was capable of showing any emotion. *Government? Shedding tears?* I could not believe it! Well, I guess *Government* is only human after all. May God bless him, I thought to myself.

I gave Dad another quick hug, pretended I never saw his tears and avoided making eye contact with him so as not to make him feel embarrassed, then I left hurriedly. I only had two small bags so I never bothered to check them in. When it was time to board the plane, Auntie Ota and I made our way towards the boarding gate.

We found our seats, sat down, got ready to take off and thoughts of my Dad flooded back. Feeling teary again, I held on to that image of him. I knew he loved us all genuinely, only something went wrong before he decided to take a second wife. What that was, I do not know. As to why *Government* would also be teary was simply beyond me. Almost everyone on the plane had noticed my Auntie try to console me, so I tried to do something or to remember a joke that could put a smile on my face to stop me from being a *cry-baby*.

What came to mind later was that Dad only shed tears because he would miss his slave and tomboy *(for there was no one else who could carry out the chores as perfectly as I did)*, and not because he would truly miss me.

Abracadabra, it worked! Cheeky me, but that sure did *slap* a smile onto my teary face! Wiping away my tears in one swipe, I transferred my thoughts from Dad to meeting James and his family.

Chapter Seven:
Meeting My Future In-Laws

O n arriving in Lagos, I told my Auntie about James and that I intended to spend my last night in Nigeria with his family. Auntie Ota was a pleasant and easy-going woman. Thankfully, she gave her consent and almost immediately, I flagged down a taxi and gave the driver James's address.

My heart sank when the taxi pulled up in front of a weather-beaten, ramshackle house. As the driver pointed to it and told me his fare, I was not only shocked, but also reluctant to get out of the taxi.

At first, I thought it was either a joke or that I had been taken to the wrong address; perhaps the driver had made a mistake. I had to check the address twice, because my expectations were very high due to James's *braggadocio* and exaggeration. At last, however, I summoned up the courage to pay the driver and managed to drag myself out of his taxi to knock on the front door.

If I was disappointed by merely seeing the exterior of the house, I was shattered when the door creaked open to admit me inside. Even so, I did not show it. Instead, I tried my hardest to conceal the extent to which I was crestfallen, making sure that not a hint of sadness was visible on my face as his family members happily welcomed me.

A big meal was prepared in my honour, *African style*. After the lovely meal, I expressed my gratitude for their warm reception and told them how pleased I was to have finally met them. I presumed the feeling was mutual as they were very friendly towards me.

His dad, now deceased *(bless his soul),* was a pensioner, aged about 90, married to two wives, and a father to more or less a dozen children. James's mother was the youngest of the wives and they all lived under one roof in a one-bedroom rented apartment in Surulere, Lagos.

During our courtship days at school, James had lied that his dad was an accountant and that he was from an affluent middle-class family. In retrospect, there were telltale signs, but I was so very much in love with him to notice them. I had been blinded by love, I guess.

Later, that evening, James took me out to visit some of his friends and he introduced me as his *wife*. Wow, this is amazingly huge! I thought to myself. After we left his friends, I told James we needed to talk. He agreed and we went to a nearby restaurant for something to drink. Without mincing my words, I told him I was very happy to see him, but that I did not appreciate the lies he had fed me while we were at school.

Poverty is not a crime, but James had no reason to lie to me because I loved him for who he was, not for what he had or what I could get from him. I wondered what he was thinking of when he had lied. Did he not intend for our relationship to be serious enough for me to find out the truth later? Was he stupid or did he think I would be foolish enough to leave the country without getting to know my future in-laws?

James admitted he had lied. He immediately fell to his knees to beg for forgiveness and was in tears as he blamed the devil. It was easy to pardon a young man who could and would humble himself before a woman, but I wondered momentarily how many more lies he had told or how well I actually knew him. I am no angel myself, I lied to him too while renewing my passport but it was necessary, as I later explained to him when I informed him of my travel.

By the time we got back to his house, most of his family members were asleep, apart from his older sister who had waited up for us. I told her about James's dishonesty and then expressed my fears and concerns. She was surprised and upset, but apologised on James's behalf before lashing out at him for his idiocy, to the point where I almost felt sorry for him. We chatted until the early hours of the morning and then prayed before finally going to bed.

I could not sleep because I had so many reservations. I was very restless as some nasty premonitions of evil were lingering in my mind. I began to ponder what to do about my discovery and prayed for God to take control, before eventually dozing off to sleep.

When my alarm woke me up at 6.00a.m., my mind was made up. I loved James and would never turn my back on him. I had thought, like every young girl in love, that maybe it was God's plan to bring me into that family to help them. As a result, I vowed to help James travel to England so he could help his family, especially his aged Dad.

My flight was at 10.00a.m. that morning. I was already awake at 6.00a.m. so I decided to get ready. James was also up and had got dressed, but he was walking around with a face like a *wet weekend*. Afterwards, we prayed with the whole family, ate breakfast, said our goodbyes and left the house just after 7.00a.m. for the airport.

On our way, James wallowed in self-pity; he was very quiet, ashamed and sad. Worse still, I saw fear in his face. He was afraid that he had lost me for good. Unable to bear the miserable look on his face, I advised him to snap out of it and to forget the past so we could start all over again with a clean slate *(year zero)*. This was on the condition that he promised never to lie to me again, no matter how good or bad the case may be.

James vowed, giving me his word that it would never happen again. Happy and satisfied, I promised to send for him as soon as I found work and was able to save up enough money for his plane ticket. That put the winning smile I loved so much back on his face and he escorted me a lot further than was normally allowed at the airport. He managed this by telling every airport staff that tried to stop him on the way at various points that I was his fiancée and he was heartbroken I was leaving without him.

His luck was soon to run out and we parted just before I had to go through security to board. It broke my heart as I tore myself from him. Blinded by tears, I slowly began walking away towards security, still looking behind and waving at James. I could see tears running down his cheeks too as he stood there, waving, not moving until I was out of sight. My only consolation was our being together in due course.

Poor James, would he be alright? How would he cope? I thought about him rather than myself and prayed for God to help me console him. My love for James was greater than life itself, regardless of my discovery.

★ ★ ★

The story about Auntie Ota, which I promised my Mum and Gloria I would fill them in on later, was simply that I lost her. After telling Auntie Ota about James on arriving in Lagos, I hailed a taxi to James's house, while Auntie Ota spent the night with a friend who was also travelling with us. We all agreed to meet at the airport the following morning and whilst I was still with James, Auntie Ota was busy chatting to her friend.

On the plane, she had swapped seats with a kind gentleman so she could sit with her friend but she occasionally checked to see if I was alright. After a while, I told her to relax and to enjoy her chitchat as I was not a baby, but an adult, which made us all laugh. They chatted until we landed and since I was very cold, I walked briskly and followed in the direction of the other passengers, leaving them behind, still chatting.

Even though I had not been in London for 17 years, I did not need anyone to hold my hand or to chaperone me. I finally lost her for good after I sighted she and her friend, both with their Nigerian passports, in the other long queue.

In all fairness, she phoned to check that I had got to my Mum's safely that day and then she visited us a week later, before going back to Nigeria. As an international businesswoman, Auntie Ota frequented the UK every couple of months. Unfortunately, we have lost contact with her and have not seen her since then.

Chapter Eight:
Blood, Sweat & Tears: James's Arrival in the United Kingdom

Settling down a couple of days after my arrival, I secured two cleaning jobs - scrubbing toilets *(just like Cinderella)* and cleaning offices. The difference was that I had love and was in love. I worked very hard to contribute towards my upkeep at home and to save money to enable James to join me in the United Kingdom.

I bought myself a cheap *make-believe* wedding ring that actually made me feel like a married woman. In spite of that, I went about my daily chores feeling sad because it seemed like part of me was missing and I vowed not to rest or be happy until James, my love, had joined me.

I am normally a very bubbly person, but at some point, my behaviour became somewhat melancholic, which did not go down well with my Mum. In addition, she knew how hard I worked, how much money I earned and exactly how much I needed to get by daily. After calculating it all mentally *(for Mum was and still is quicker than Einstein ever was wherever money is concerned),* she wanted to know what I did with the rest of my money.

When I first arrived, the three of us had a family meeting. It was decided that I would give Mum any money I had left after my expenses, when I got a job. Gloria was already doing this and this was also fine by me. The reason was so Mum could pay the bills, provide our food and then send the rest of the money over to be used for my siblings' education and living expenses in Nigeria. Unfortunately, that was not the case when I finally secured my jobs. I did not *surrender* the bulk of my wages and Mum noticed.

She somehow found out about James and concluded that I was saving some money aside to bring him over. Mum became enraged, as she could not understand how I could have fallen in love so easily and that I intended to marry someone I barely knew. She was so disgusted she began to think that James had used some African voodoo on me, as this was not the same Irene, her daughter. 'If that was not the case', Mum said, 'Why would you not think about helping your own siblings back home first? How long have you known him, two months?' She asked, *spitting feathers* and then continued, 'You can't have known him that long because you always tell me everything. How well do you know him? Most African men are all the same, just like your Father', she blurted out angrily *(remembering Dad's deeds, the thought of James annoyed her immensely and it all became too much for me to bear).* That's Mum, the semi-disciplinarian, hardly ever annoyed, but when angry, you sure know about it.

Mum did not speak to me for days. I felt alienated and was all by myself. Every morning on our way to work *(we all left home together in the mornings),* Gloria and Mum walked side by side, chatting away, while I tagged along behind them. Feeling alone and neglected, I could not bear the fact that my own family could behave in such a manner, so I had to try to resolve the situation.

Speaking to Gloria shortly after, I found out that she was caught in the middle. We both planned to speak to Mum together and I organised a family meeting the next day.

In presenting my case, I pleaded with Mum to try to understand that I loved James. Furthermore, I added that when she had the opportunity to meet and get to know him, she would find out what an absolute angel he was and therefore would gain a son. I then made a promise that as soon as James arrived, both of us would work very hard to raise enough money to send for my siblings who would be present at our wedding. Little did I know that with Mum's age and wisdom, even if I climbed Mount Everest or an *'Iroko'* tree, I would be unable to see what she could see, sat down *(An African adage).*

By putting it like that, Mum had no choice but to reluctantly agree due to her love for me, and I was glad. I later celebrated James's birthday in his absence, while he travelled from Lagos to Benin to be with the rest of my siblings and organised parties to celebrate both my birthday and graduation.

Subsequent to that, James and his family went to see my family for a formal introduction. As preparation for a proposed marriage, it is a customary requirement for the families of couples intending to get married to meet formally. This is to ascertain that both families consent to the union as it is extremely necessary for them to give their official consent.

On hearing the news, I was elated and I happily informed a couple of friends about the formal introduction that took place in my absence. However, I soon became sad when they teased and made fun of me instead, stating that I was *James's ticket* to the UK. I disagreed by insisting his love for me was genuine and said that not only was he a devout Christian, he had no knowledge of me being a British citizen when we became lovers.

The main reason I went to great lengths to defend James was to erase those awful thoughts from their minds since I did not think what they were saying about him was true. I only informed James of my British status as I was preparing for my trip to the United Kingdom. Due to their sarcastic remarks, I never spoke to those girls again. They were deleted from my diary and life.

Despite the distance between us, I loved and trusted James very much. My mind was at ease because I believed that since he had the fear of God in him and he loved me, he would never deceive, cheat or lie to me again. Those thoughts kept me going and made me stronger, but his absence created a growing void in me by the day, which I tried to fill by working very hard. How can someone miss a fellow human being so much?

Working conscientiously from 4.00a.m. in the morning until *(stupid o'clock)* very late at night, I was, for the first time, truly able to save a considerable amount of money to get someone to assist with the processing of James's trip to the UK. As fate would have it, an ex-colleague of mine called Lady Gee, who I trusted with the money I laboured so hard for, duped me. I never saw nor heard from this woman again, who had assured me she would successfully assist with procuring James a visa.

According to her, she was a regular traveller who understood the ins and outs of foreign travels. She must have sensed that I was stupid, gullible and desperate and then cashed in on it. This dubious act broke my heart, but not for long. My love for James was so great that the anguish I felt only made me more determined to bring James to the UK at any cost and I worked harder towards achieving my goal.

On the second attempt, which was one year after I had arrived in the UK, I tried to sort things out myself. After forwarding all the necessary documents to the Home Offices in both London and Nigeria, my application was successful and James was finally granted a visa to the UK. 'Hurrah!' I exclaimed, as I threw a punch into the air with my right fist when I received the news. I then sent him some money to purchase his plane ticket to England and for the necessary things required for the journey. My joy was beyond comprehension.

* * *

It was Sunday November 25, 1990, the day of James's arrival and I was ecstatic. 'I'm so happy', I exclaimed to Gloria and her boyfriend Segun *(now her husband),* while we were on our way to pick James up from Heathrow Airport. The weather was cold but amazingly sunny for that time of year. I was literally *walking on air* and I could not wait for the moment when I saw James and could run into his arms, gleefully laughing.

Words could not describe my joy. My palms were wet despite the cold, and it felt like summer to me. I was almost oblivious to the entire human and industrial bustle around me at the airport. My body was shaking, as I was nervous, anxious and ecstatic all at the same time. I did not recall the nightmare I had endured when I arrived at Heathrow a year ago and my main concern was waiting to welcome my James.

My face lit up like a beam of light and my heart skipped a beat the moment I spotted James walking towards us. He looked thin, older and emaciated; not quite like when I last saw him, and his shoes looked like they had seen forty miles of bad road. Yet, his smile and good looks were still intact.

He must have had a hard time without me. *Not to worry, Big Momma will soon change all that with her delicious dishes,* I smiled, thinking about what Gloria had said to me when I arrived. *I will fatten him up. As for his shoes, they belong in a museum* I thought, still smiling as I ran up to James.

I flung myself into his open arms with which he embraced me and we both had tears of joy in our eyes as I gave him the biggest hug and the longest kiss in history. My dream had come true at last.

After introducing him to Gloria and Segun *(not that that was necessary, since they already felt like they knew James as I talked about him all the time),* we took the Tube back to our house so James could meet Mum. On the way,

Segun and James started chatting so quickly and easily that you would think they had known each other all their life. In our absence, Mum had no choice but to prepare for James's arrival as she knew how much I loved him and how happy I was.

We arrived home and as soon as James saw Mum, he immediately threw himself to the floor to greet her in prostration. That did it for Mum! She saw how respectful, cheerful and courteous he was and she could see why I loved him. Mum served us the specially prepared meal of pounded yam and tantalising spinach *(egusi)* soup that was littered with stockfish, beef and tilapia fish. She had made it earlier in honour of James and we all sat down at the table to eat the scrumptious meal.

Prior to James's arrival, I had rented and furnished a flat for him, bought the necessary items needed to make a comfy home and secured a job for him. After we had eaten, I asked for Mum's permission to take James to the flat, as I intended to spend the night there to help him unpack his personal effects and to help him *settle* in. Mum agreed.

That night, our first night together in London was nothing but total bliss. If only walls could talk. It was a November to remember! I was complete. I became whole and alive again.

★ ★ ★

Despite spending most of my time with James after work, I returned home at night, without fail, as I was still living with my Mum and Gloria.

James was so charming and respectful that everyone close to me soon grew to love him too. He settled in very well and acclimatised a lot quicker than I had expected. After a while, we went to our local council office to put our names on a waiting list to register for a more cost-effective home of our own.

From jumping off the bus and getting to James's flat, which would normally require a 10-minute walk, yet always seemed like two minutes to me, as I waltzed or ran down the street to his flat, singing and smiling to myself while savouring in advance, the joy of being alone with him. My heart filled with happiness just thinking about James.

'Hi honey, I'm home!' I would call out to him from downstairs as soon as I entered the flat. I knew his work schedule better than he did and I always knew when he was or should be home. I had my own set of keys to open his front door and on hearing my voice James would emerge from his bedroom or another place in the flat and spread out his arms for me to *rumba* into his warm embrace.

'How was work today, honey?' He would ask, taking off my coat.

'Fine, honey, thanks, and how was yours? How much did you miss me?' I would often quiz him.

'Loads', he would reply. I loved James so much. Life was great and we were very happy together.

'I missed you too.'

'You were a little late in coming.'

'I thought I should put in some overtime to earn some extra pounds. Do you remember my promise to Mum regarding my siblings?' I had explained it to him carefully and lovingly when he first arrived and he was cool with it. 'We need the money, don't you think so darling?'

'Yeah, I do, but give yourself a break please. Slow down a bit, right?' James said as he held me close to surround me with his endless love.

I simply nodded, looking at him coquettishly. Such words from James put me on cloud nine and assured me of nothing else but his love.

We then talked some more about a whole range of issues - the future, launching joint businesses and having kids one day. Regarding the latter, he always sang these words to me (his version of The Beatles - Take Good Care of My Baby). *You will take good care of my son; please don't ever let him cry, please. I... love... babies.'* The song constantly made me cry.

Curiously, I would sometimes ask him, 'How do you know we are going to have a son, what if it is a girl?'

'Oh no, no, no! We are very strong men in our lineage; I can only produce strong sons, so, a son it shall be!' He would answer, flexing his muscles. I was full of smiles and happiness. James was so very witty and sweet. He continued. 'You saw for yourself that there were a lot of young boys running around when you visited us in Naija. Whose kids do you think they were? Our neighbours?'

'Not yours, I hope?' I said, pulling my face and looking as if I was angry. The truth was, that was very far from how I felt.

'Nah, you see, we have more males than females in my family and we are very strong. Dad is still going strong at over 90 years old which should say a lot about me.' James said, winking, smiling and desiring me with *his come to bed eyes*. I smiled back. Words could not express the love I have for this man. He is my drug.

Chapter Nine:
Encounter With An Angel
(Auntie Pat)

Walking side by side with James's loving and powerful arms around me, we strolled to Dalston Market. It was a fine spring afternoon and while we were window-shopping, James said he had seen a woman he thought looked familiar.

'Really, are you sure?' I asked him. I was inquisitive. A woman who looks familiar to James in London? By now, I had restrained and slowed him down, holding him by the arm as I whirled him round gently towards me, searching his face for a hidden clue.

He was not very sure, so he said, 'I don't know. It was such a long time ago and I am not absolutely certain now.'

'Go and speak to her, then ask her if she's the one', I said and nudged him forward.

James thought she resembled Pat, the sister of his best friend Clem, who he knew was living in London, but had not seen for a long time.

'Go on', I insisted as he was still hesitating, 'what have you got to lose? She can only say yes or no.' James was a very shy guy and would not go, so I walked up to her as she was looking at a fuchsia pink blouse and said, 'Hi, please excuse me, are you Clement's sister?'

Surprised, she looked at me while also trying to figure out who I was, and then she mouthed a hesitant, 'Yes?' wondering who this stranger in front of her could be.

James joined us as I was speaking to her and I introduced him saying, 'James, my boyfriend is your bro...' Before I could finish my sentence, she gave James a big hug and then yelled, 'James, you are here! Am I seeing clearly?'

'Yes, of course you are.' James replied coolly, as he took off his signature dark glasses for a minute, only to put them back on, smiling underneath them. Just as I was starting to feel like a *lemon,* the woman also hugged me excitedly, then turned to James again saying, 'It's wonderful to see you here, James.'

'Well, you have me to thank for that', I said jokingly. 'You know he is a shy bloke. He was reluctant to find out if it was you he had seen so I took it upon myself to come over to you.'

'Aw, bless your beautiful heart, sister. Thank you very much, I really appreciate that.'

Afterwards, we exchanged our contact details and a beautiful family friendship was born. This is one I am particularly grateful for because Auntie Pat is an amazingly genuine woman and a Godsend. Ever since then, we have been steadfast friends and we have shared, and are still sharing memorable magic moments together.

We were overjoyed when, after several months of our names being on the council's waiting list, with Auntie Pat's help, the council finally allocated us a flat of our own. James and I moved in and together, we set up our first proper home in Bermondsey, South East London.

Chapter Ten:
Loved Up & Engaged

J ames and I talked about getting engaged a few months later in June and on the following Saturday we went window-shopping. I was very excited and we had a wonderful experience browsing lovely jewellery shops for my engagement ring.

We saw a couple of gorgeous rings, but the prices were a little on the high side and beyond our budget. I got a bit panicky because I thought we were never going to be able to afford one, and then I began to wonder whether we really needed a ring.

Fortunately, we eventually found one that we both fell in love with, after searching more thoroughly. Luckily, it was available in my size, although it cost slightly more than we had originally budgeted for. A silver ring inlaid with gold, it was!

Loved up, we left the shop hand in hand, bought some Kentucky Fried Chicken and strolled to a nearby park to eat it. After we had finished eating, James got up. I did likewise *(thinking we were going home so he could do the honourable thing of asking me to be his wife)*, but I was surprised when he got down on one knee, to put the ring on the finger of my left hand as he asked me to marry him.

In full view of so many people he had knelt down for me. My goodness, was I embarrassed? This guy would kill me with his love! I was very nervous. Everyone was starring at us. My hands were shaking as I blushed, nodding my head in answer to his question and then, I said…'YES!' Looking at James's beautiful ring on my finger, I was so happy. In fact, I cried out with joy. I was engaged.

It was official between us and I had a lovely ring to show for it! Certainly not the inexpensive one I had bought for myself, which should be kept in a museum as a souvenir alongside his 40 miles of bad road shoes *(if it were possible)*, to show our kids one day. *To be fair, the cheap ring served its purpose and it would be unfair to knock it now. The shoes? Long gone!*

★ ★ ★

We set the date of our wedding within two weeks of our engagement for December 21, 1991. This gave us the time we needed to save up more money since we would be footing the wedding bill ourselves. Fortunately, we had been putting some savings aside for that purpose for a while, in fact, since we decided to get married after James's arrival.

Our wedding was only six months away. The thought of it all was so scary because I was starting out into the great unknown with James. Like every young woman, it is always daunting to imagine what the unfamiliar journey of marriage will bring. Amidst all the pomp and pageantry of preparation, build-ups and incidents that lead-up to the marriage ceremony, there regularly comes a moment of truth when you come to terms with the fact that you are truly leaving your family and becoming part of another one.

The sobering reality is that I would now be entrusting my future to a stranger. Yet, the comforting and most important fact is that this future would be spent with the man I love and could not live without, which makes it more exciting. Although, in my opinion, the best thing by far about getting married is making a promise before God; to love and remain faithful to each other forever.

I could not think of much else other than planning and organising my big day. From the age of twelve, I had not only dreamt of marrying my Prince Charming, but also envisioned what my wedding dress and day would be like. My thoughts went out to my parents and I prayed that James would never do to me what my Dad did to my Mum by marrying another wife. 'Anyway, we are in England', I reassured myself, 'that would not happen!' James had never been ashamed or even flinched at the idea of kneeling down in public; which he had done for me once way back in Nigeria and then again here in London.

What else could I want or wish for from a man who adores his woman? If I had had any reservations about whether James loved me, that skepticism simply vanished at this thought. I therefore erased all the other silly thoughts, doubts and fears about him from my mind and concentrated on the task at hand.

I was so excited. I set a budget with my good friend Felicia, Mum and Gloria, so I could figure out the exact cost for everything and how much money we needed. James and I chose the church we wanted to be married in and with bags of energy to spare, I went about booking the church, the reception venue, photographers, venue decorators, etc., and gradually crossed things off my *to do* list. I was buzzing and I totally enjoyed making all the necessary arrangements.

I kept my part of the bargain that I had made with Mum. My Dad and siblings from my Mum arrived from Nigeria several weeks before the wedding, which meant that my parents, my brothers and sisters, friends and a few extended family members, were all going to witness our joyous occasion. I was ecstatic and felt like the luckiest bride-to-be in the whole, wide world.

★ ★ ★

A friend of mine who got married a few weeks after my engagement agreed to lend me her wedding gown, veil and silk flowers for a small fee, but I had to dry-clean the gown before and after use. I chose my elder sister Christine as my maid of honour, my other sisters Gloria, Michelle, Gezza, and my cousin Orobosa as my bridesmaids. The cute little flower girl and ring-bearer were my friend's children, and they were all very happy and excited to be part of the bridal party. James chose his friend Tony, who is also the husband of my very good friend Serena as his best man, with my brothers Max and Michael as his groomsmen.

Having gained first-hand experience in purchasing my engagement ring, we had an idea of what we wanted for our wedding rings. *We knew what to expect too.* After visiting a number of jewellery shops, we eventually chose a gold set of lovely *his 'n' hers* matching wedding bands. Unfortunately, our chosen one was unavailable in my size. I have quite big fingers and the ones for women were rather thinner and smaller than the men's for obvious reasons.

Luckily for me, my size was available in the men's band and I was happy to purchase it straightaway. Besides, I prefer my rings broader and bigger. However, there was a slight problem. It was more expensive at almost double the price.

I was gutted, so I haggled with the sales assistant in order to reduce the price since it was due to no fault of mine that my size was not in stock. He apologised, although he would not budge on the price, stating he was not in a position to reduce it. Then he mentioned that the shop could order my size within 28 days.

'Twenty-eight days?' I was almost shouting, wide-eyed and surprised. 'What a joke!' For all I cared, the poor shop assistant might as well have said *28 years!* I was not prepared to wait that long. *I wanted the ring yesterday. Doesn't he understand that I'm in love?* Moreover, I had already lost interest in the women's design. Since it was now possible to get the men's band which I not only loved, but also now desired, I had to get it!

All the while James barely spoke. Apart from expressing his surprise at my haggling skills and muttering the words, *'You are doing just fine all by yourself honey, any interference from me might make it worse, so carry on, good girl'*, he left it all to me. That, I gladly took as a compliment and my confidence increased.

I was getting nowhere fast with the assistant so I requested to speak to the manager who confirmed what the sales assistant had said. Yet, the Virgo in me refused to accept any negative response. I pointed out to him that as the manager he should be able to use his discretion or I would take my business elsewhere. After a little more persuasion, he yielded by knocking a whopping 40% off the tag price and I only ended up paying £5 extra, which was next to nothing. Ecstatic, I performed my happy dance.

Who says being persistent when haggling never pays off? I was so happy, I planted a smacker on the manager's left cheek, while James gave him a brisk handshake. Honestly, because I loved the ring that much, I would have paid the difference in price, but there is no harm in either trying to pay less by being cheeky or even pushing my luck. The worst-case scenario would have been a big fat *'no'* but, thank God, that was not the case. James and I had matching wedding rings and I had got a cracking deal, happy days!

With the ring matter sorted out, we headed to the printers for our wedding invitation cards. After going through an avalanche of designs and invitation wordings, colours, styles of calligraphy and their prices, we chose what we thought was perfect for us and ordered a hundred cards to be printed.

Generally, with regards to most Nigerian occasions, an invitation card is not always necessary. In some cases *(especially weddings)*, just a simple word of mouth invitation, stating the basic information; the three W's *(what, where and when)*, will normally suffice. For this reason, it is always better to multiply the number of invited guests by three. Invite one person and three will turn up since Nigerians are very friendly and welcoming individuals. We therefore were to expect no less than a minimum of 300 guests. *Nowadays, some Nigerians are a lot less liberal and more precise regarding invitees.*

It was a long day and James was feeling exhausted. He was not familiar with the elaborate planning and organising involved in a wedding, and neither was I, but I was in such a *happy* mood that I enjoyed every bit of it. Every woman in love dreams and looks forward to her wedding day and plans it with joy and excitement. Hence, I happily sorted out most of our wedding arrangements with occasional input from James.

Our wedding theme was a combination of our favourite colours for the bridal party and decorations. James and his groomsmen decided to hire dark evening suits and matching top hats. Our choice of cake was a lovely three-tiered sponge and fruit.

Mum was in charge of organising the catering. We discussed a wide variety of delicious, mouth-watering Nigerian dishes, which were to be prepared and cooked by my relatives. Felicia was responsible for the English finger buffet food. The music DJ, photographers and videographers were all booked and paid for. Due to the large quantity of drinks to be purchased, we shopped around for special offers and gradually bought a wide variety of soft and alcoholic drinks at good bargain prices.

The invitation cards were ready by the middle of September and I was unbelievably excited about seeing our names in print. We both filled in the names and addresses of our invitees and posted them out in October.

Everything was ready and paid for by the end of November, after which I felt hugely relieved and then there was an interval. I soon got bored of the lull, missing all the stress and excitement. I had enjoyed it when everyone in our household and family was abuzz with the preparation and arrangements for my wedding. All the same, I was happy. The most important things had been sorted out, crossed off and then ticked as done on my *to-do* list.

★ ★ ★ .

Three weeks before our wedding day, Dad asked a few very close friends and family members to attend a get-together. It was for an informal introduction before the big day at 4.00p.m. the following Sunday. James's only relative in the UK lived in Kent but he was happy to represent his Dad.

My sisters, Mum and I went shopping to purchase the items needed on the eve of the introduction. On Sunday morning, James and I arrived at my Mum's house very early to begin the preparations and to make sure everything was ready before our guests arrived.

Predictably, none of our guests arrived at 4.00p.m., the time stated for the commencement of the gathering *(this was due to the phenomenon called African time, which has nothing to do with watches or clocks. Most Africans will usually arrive late to any occasion, regardless of what time the event has been billed to start).*

Some guests arrived later than others, but everyone that had been invited was present and seated by 6.00p.m. *(two solid hours behind schedule). Jeez, I thought!* After the prayers, the introduction took place. Everyone introduced themselves and James declared his intentions again, followed by the acknowledgements.

There was a huge array of food and drinks available for everyone. Segun, Gloria's heartthrob, served as the Master of Ceremonies; making everyone roar with laughter with snippets of information, riddles and jokes.

He had created suspense right from the start by asking what James and I, or any other person in the room would do, if they had a child who did what he would say, only at the end of his session. However, when he finished, Segun himself had forgotten to mention what the child did.

'So, what did the child do?' *Government* reminded him. It was very unusual for Dad to be interested in something like this, but he was in a particularly good mood that day.

'Oh yes, thank you, Dad', Segun said, who had begun to address *Government* this way a while ago. He then quickly dashed to the corner where the sound system was softly playing a number by Gregory Isaacs called *Night Nurse,* and reduced the volume of the music.

'Aha, everybody, please listen to this', said Segun, trying to get everyone's attention.

'You have an eight-year-old daughter. Your family friend, a couple, came to visit and brought along with them a bunch of ripe plantains as a gift for you. When your wife told you there was no food in the house to feed your guests, you asked her to fry the plantains that the guests had brought with them. She fried all the plantains and fed the guests who ate them all up and burped satisfactorily as they left. Immediately after, your little girl sidled up to you and cooed into your ear saying, 'Dad, they brought the plantains in their car and took them away in their bellies.'

Before Segun could ask the guests again what each of them would do to such a girl if he or she had her as their daughter, a thunderous roar of laughter erupted that only began to calm down some three minutes later. This provoked many varying reactions from our guests.

The first joke Segun *cracked* was equally as funny. He simply walked into the middle of the living room after an elder had said the opening prayer and without so much as introducing himself, began narrating a story.

'A couple had a misunderstanding four days after their wedding and so they refused to talk to each other. By the fourth day of their malice, the husband got tired of it all, but did not know what to do to win his wife back. On the fifth day, he rose from the bed and began searching for something in the house. He knelt down to look under the bed and then lifted up the bed sheets, opened the wardrobes and drawers and slammed them shut, frustrated. After an hour of the drama, his wife could bear it no longer and she barked at him, 'What on earth are you looking for?'

'Ah', he heaved a sigh of relief, 'I've found it.'

'You have found what?' The wife said stiffly, still very angry.

'I've found your voice at last.'

The guests burst into the first paroxysms of laughter, just like the woman in the story, and in the middle of the excitement Segun announced, 'My name is Segun... I will be the Programme Conductor for this Introduction Ceremony. I pray that James and Irene, who we are gathered here for today, will not be like the couple in this story, amen.' There was hysterical laughter from all present.

Thereafter, some guests stood up to tell different jokes and one guest narrated a first-ever telephone conversation between a rich, but illiterate man in Nigeria *(nicknamed Mr. Moneymisroad)* and his son in London.

Dad *(Mr. Moneymisroad)*: 'Ello, ello, is that *London?*'

Son: 'Hello, I can't hear you properly, who is this please? Dad, is that you?'

Dad repeated: 'Ello is that *London?*' Trying to spell London, he said, 'Elu for Eluphant, O for Under, Eni for Anything? Then he continued, 'Osagie' *(son's name)*, 'werni-khin-ar' *(the Bini translation for)* 'is that you?' He later waved his hands in the air as he saluted his son via the telephone. Everyone burst out laughing again.

They were totally in stitches, as another guest asked, 'Is pooh-pooh one word or two?'

No one could think clearly enough to figure out the answer to the question. That was to be expected, bearing in mind that most of them were either a little tipsy, a tad too merry or simply just drunk from all the excitement and happiness. Still, they saw the funny side of it all and at the time, there was not a dry eye in the house.

We had so much fun and we enjoyed ourselves amidst the jokes, dancing, eating and drinking. The merriment finally ended a little after 11.00p.m. It was a good introduction party. My family wished our guests and would-be in-law a happy night's rest, promising in the process to see them on the day of the wedding.

Our wedding rehearsals took place a week before the big day and everyone in the bridal party attended. Gloria and Segun threw a stag party for James on the eve of our wedding day. Afterwards, he spent the night at Segun's as it is believed to be bad luck for the groom to see his bride before the marriage ceremony.

★ ★ ★

On the morning of my wedding day I felt very nervous, as though there were a thousand butterflies in my stomach. I got up to take a long bath to calm my nerves, after which I felt better. Gezza made me some food and while I was eating, Auntie Pat walked in with her large make-up box. She got to work on me as soon as I had finished my food and in no time at all, she had me all dolled up.

My bridesmaids arrived shortly after Auntie Pat and there was a bit of juggling with the dresses among the owners, even though they all had nametags on them. Mum, on the other hand, was in panic mode. She was stressed out because one of the dishes could not be made due to a missing vital ingredient. I ignored them all as I did not want to be bothered unnecessarily. I had heard a lot about what misunderstandings and disunity there could be during wedding preparations.

★ ★ ★

The two wedding cars arrived and Dad called out to us just as we were putting the finishing touches to our make-up. Afterwards, we all made our way to the chauffeur-driven silver Mercedes-Benz that had been fabulously decorated with lovely white ribbons and bows. Dad, Christine, my maid of honour and I, drove to the church in one car, while the rest of my bridal party went in the other.

Chapter Eleven:
A Dream Come True

Our wedding venue was at St. Giles Church in Camberwell, South East London. Auntie Pat had done a good job. I could see that as I stole a look at myself in the car's wing mirror *(despite being in front of the massive mirror in my room for over an hour, I needed to reassure myself once again by checking this car's little wing mirror)*. 'Perfect, but hmm, how vain I am!' I said, loving what I saw in the mirror and smiling to myself.

Auntie Pat had ensured I was the prettiest bride in town, by perfectly applying my make-up and dressing me beautifully. Felicia also did all that was necessary to ensure the occasion went as well as I had planned.

At the altar, James stood in his hired tuxedo suit, with a cane and top hat to match. He placed the hat under his arm, smiled at me and whispered, 'I love you. Honey, you look very lovely', into my ear, as I stood by his side. On hearing that I felt great, as well as beautiful in my hired white long flowing Chantilly lace gown, fully decorated with tiny white beads and diamante stones. It was finished off with a matching white veil on my head that trailed long enough to form an elongated train *(but certainly not cathedral long)*.

'I love you too honey.' I blushed and smiled as the Officiant started the service. Then, at the very heart of the ceremony, during the exchanging of our vows, a bad cough overwhelmed me. I started coughing so hard, without stopping and there were tears in my eyes. The more I tried to hold it back, the more I coughed. It was so embarrassing that Mum quickly got up to get me a glass of water to drink before the cough gradually subsided.

Goodness gracious! Talk about an interruption or divine intervention; any just cause, or rather impediments as to why these persons should not...? Perhaps *fate* was trying to warn me against someone or something.

Immediately after the Officiant pronounced us 'man and wife' we sealed it with a kiss as everyone cheered. At the end of the church service, we walked lovingly towards the congregation with our procession in tow. We had huge smiles on our faces as our guests congratulated us. I was so happy, it would have taken surgery to remove the smiles from my face the next day. Shortly after, we made our way outside the church, ready for our Kodak moment. Briefly, I mentally rhapsodised about the music track entitled *Magic Moments* by the group, Lakeside. I thought to myself that if James continued to make things better for me, inferring from The Whispers's musical track, *I Can Make It Better,* then, his wish would be my command, remembering another Lakeside music track, *Your Wish Is My Command.*

After the photo session, we were chauffeur-driven to the reception venue, which was packed full with our guests awaiting the lovely bride and the lucky groom. We had a standing ovation as we danced into the hall, making quite a spectacular and colourful entrance with our bridal entourage. Thereafter, we were ushered to our seats as the newest married couple in town.

The Chairperson of the occasion said the prayers and the Master of Ceremonies *(not Segun, but a relative of mine)* supervised the cake cutting, proposed a toast to us and gave a short speech.

Mum and her friends gathered on the dance floor to dance and sing in our traditional Edo dialect. They sang songs of blessings, some of which were about being fruitful in marriage and seeing our children's children. It was a wonderful and glorious day. The ceremony was beautiful, our guests had great fun and there was an abundance of food and drinks.

After our wedding, we could not afford a honeymoon, so James and I took a week off work and we stayed at home to relax. I was content and satisfied.

James was very loving. We spent most of our waking moments in each other's arms and did nothing but make love, eat, sleep, rest, and we sometimes strolled to the park or to the cinema. We opened most of our presents on the second week of our marriage and I wished our beautiful life would last forever. 'Love is, and should indeed be forever', I mused, smiling to myself.

Chapter Twelve:
The Cracks Cometh

After James and I were married, I organised a high profile art exhibition for James a few weeks later at the prestigious Whiteleys Shopping Centre - Bayswater. It was his debut. The aim was to exhibit his art works from Nigeria and it was a chance to plug some sales too. The proceeds taken on the day were not great, but all I wanted was for him to gain some exposure as an artist, which was more important. Following that, I enrolled at college for a computing course to upgrade my computer and IT skills.

Juggling both work and college was not easy for me. What's more, James later quit his full-time job for a part-time one due to some flimsy excuses. He began to display his true colours and things were not as rosy as they had seemed or as I had imagined our life to be. A cycle of two-timing, late nights out, shameless lies, emotional abuse, drug abuse and drunkenness all followed in quick succession.

Gradually, he started staying out late after work and there came a point when he was hardly ever at home. I remember spending one particular long night waiting for him to come home. When he finally appeared after 3.00a.m., I asked him, 'Honey, where have you been after work and all night? Don't I, at least, deserve a phone call from you so I know you are okay?'

'Oh, just out with my mates', he mumbled casually.

James eventually lost his part-time job, started smoking cigarettes and then graduated to marijuana *(weed, wakibaki or whatever it was, and to date, I still do not know)*. I was shocked beyond belief. To me, James, a devout Christian, never smoked or drank *(except he hid those habits well and were among the lies and secrets I never knew about him in Nigeria)*. For an amateur drinker, his favourite lager 'Special Brew' *aka 'Gut Rot' or 'Tramp Juice'*, Alcohol by volume *(ABV) 9.0%*, is made of very strong stuff. This drink is lethal on its own let alone when combined with wakibaki or other.

It was obvious and heartbreaking to see that James was headed for a downward spiral. Nevertheless, I loved him so much and pined for him in his absence. I would sometimes wait *(no matter how hungry I was, or how late it was)*, until he got home before we ate supper together.

His excuses for staying out late at this point switched from the need to hunt for a job to hustling, which resulted in nothing. I was naive enough to believe him, as he had become a pathological liar who lied as a default action.

However, I had my suspicions. Apart from his boozing and smoking, I knew that something was not quite right. My instincts, *not paranoia,* are very powerful. I had the sense that he was possibly up to no good while out regularly till very late, gallivanting with his mates and other women. I could literally see them laughing and making a mockery of me, while I waited *(sometimes in hunger, worry or panic)* for him to come home before I ate. Any wonder that he often did not eat when he came home because he had, most probably, already filled his belly and much more.

Despite my *gut* feelings, I was too grief-stricken to act upon them. I simply discounted them and chose to ignore the very early warning signs. I was living in denial, refusing to believe the fact that he may be cheating on me. Although, I could see what was happening from what had started as slight adjustments in his behaviour, to the extreme pattern of changes taking place.

While musing about it all and thinking about the cold shoulder he sometimes gave me on the few occasions he was around, I began to see cracks appearing on the walls of our marriage. Just as Job said in the Bible, 'What I greatly feared' *(in my case, the collapse of my marriage)*, 'had come upon me.'

It soon began to dawn on me that I had made a blunder by marrying James. My hopes and dreams of pure marital bliss were shattered and even through rose-tinted glasses, I began to realise that our love was one-sided. *Or was I wrong? I would often think along these lines and I soon began to cry myself to sleep at night.*

James had totally changed from the man I once knew him to be. Sowing seeds of doubt in my mind, I often wondered if this was the James I loved and had longed for. The same James who travelled all the way from

Lagos to Benin to celebrate both my graduation and birthday parties in my absence.

It was certainly not the James who, while putting a ring on my finger during our engagement, knelt down to declare his love publicly for me, and once before that too.

It must be a different James for whom I had humbled myself *(for the sake of urgency and quick cash)*, to take on the lowest and dirtiest of menial jobs and worked my fingers to the bone.

Whatever happened to James, the shy guy? The innocent God-fearing lad? It was indeed unbelievable!

On several occasions he returned home late, drunk, high as a kite and reeked of marijuana, wakibaki or weed. Causing sensory overload, the weed stench was so strong that I could taste it and it was probably enough to *conk* out the whole neighbourhood. When he urinated, his bladder opened like a tropical monsoon and worst of all, it smelt as if a sewage pipe had burst.

He stopped attending church because he could not be bothered with having to get up again, after dragging himself home in the early hours of Sunday morning. Even as I watched all of this happening, I could not do anything but question him. He was always very dismissive and his reply was constantly, 'You are nagging me too much. Nagging, nagging, all the time.'

My love for James was still so very strong. It took a while to believe he could do anything to hurt me and I kept tricking myself into believing that things would improve. I constantly covered up for him to prevent my few friends and relatives from finding out what was really happening.

The only opportunities I had to empty or check his pockets were before I washed or hung his clothes up in the wardrobe. I never deliberately checked his pockets, fearing what I may discover. Even if I did find anything incriminating, I would convince myself to believe the opposite. So what was the point in snooping?

Woe is me, for love truly is blind! Blind and foolish to the extent that I chose to ignore the evidence staring me in the face, such as finding a different coloured lipstick stain on his collar. Rather than believing what the truth really was, I would deceive myself into thinking it was from me *(even though I have never used an orange lipstick in my life)*.

What's more, I would disregard the unfamiliar names and contact numbers that I found in his pockets. Also, I would be too scared to investigate or call the numbers, fearing I might find out about the other woman. I dreaded the thought of James telling me, *'I'm in love with the other woman'*, as in Ray Parker Jnr's song. The thought was scary and I would immediately dismiss any negative thoughts by making myself believe they were only his friends or just the contact numbers of his associates.

One day I found an unused condom in his trouser pocket which shocked me beyond belief. For a moment I held the condom in my right hand and my mind simply went blank in our bedroom. As usual, he was out. Was I seeing things? Well, there was no way for him to wriggle out of this. I had caught him red-handed.

When James came home, I asked him about it and he looked at me with disgust, wondering what business of mine it was to be checking his pockets in the first place. Then he came up with the dumbest excuse ever, saying it belonged to my brother, Max, who had asked James to look after it for him. 'What do you know?' He said, and I believed him. He made me think that it was all in my imagination and that there was nothing wrong, because according to *His Royal Highness,* I was a fool.

I was too ashamed and embarrassed to ask Max about the condom at the time. Moreover, I did not want to talk to my siblings about matters between James and I. He had denied it. Better forgotten, I reasoned.

★ ★ ★

Quite recently, while briefing Max and Mum about this book, I happened to remember the condom issue, which is now some 20 years ago. I jokingly asked Max about the matter and his reply was, 'Sis, James was the married one, while I was young, free and single. Therefore, why on earth would I give a wedded man a condom to look after?

Even if I was wearing trousers without pockets, I would not dream of giving or asking him to keep a condom in his pocket for me. On the other hand, was I armless so that I could not carry or keep a condom in my hand? Did his excuse sound valid then? Did what he said make any sense to you, Sis?'

Max was indeed correct and I thought so too at the time, but when I confronted James about it then, he said I was a fool. I remember the exact year *(1992),* just a year after our wedding. Not only was I in denial then, I also struggled with self-doubt in the sense that I was not sure I knew what was wrong or right. I was in *love*.

★ ★ ★

After a while, it all got too much for me and I decided not to bury my head in the sand or wallow in self-pity any longer. Who was I kidding? This was my marriage, my happiness and future. I had to say or do something to take control before it was too late or got out of hand. So I made a conscious decision to snap out of whatever denial I was in or what self-doubt I had or thought I had.

I thought long and hard, and then wondered why James loved being away from his matrimonial home as much as he did and why he returned at *ridiculous o'clock* at night. To the best of my knowledge, I had done the best I could for him. My loyalty and love for him were never in doubt. I kept our home nice. I had always been and still am a good cook. I tried my best to help, advise and encourage him like a brother, to do better, without nagging *(although I couldn't open my mouth without him accusing me of nagging him)*.

I tried to be the three important things a wife should be for her husband; a lady in the living room, a good cook in the kitchen and a whore in the bedroom... Well, I might not have been the best, but I had tried to be all of these things for James until he started coming home late at night.

What was he doing out there? What else did he want? I was dying to know. I wished someone would tell me. Was he living a double life? If he was hustling or job hunting shouldn't there be at least something to show for it sometimes? It would not have surprised me if his CV also stated *married but looking,* under the *marital status*!

To be honest, he occasionally brought home some money, which was ludicrously paltry. Nonetheless, what ate away at me was his blasé attitude towards looking for any work or rather, the fact that he bluntly refused to work. *To have been looking for a job for over a year and still be empty-handed is totally beyond me.*

James never once attempted to further his career as an artist or the quick-footed athlete that he was. Neither had he handled a brush to paint or draw since he arrived. As an able-bodied man without any disabilities, James refused to find a job and he often stated, 'How much can they pay me, working?' Regularly bragging about how he could use his brains to earn millions. I waited patiently, but in vain for the Einstein in him to jump up one day and shout, *Eureka!* What was he waiting for? What was the reason for my Einstein's delay? I would have preferred him to get on with it *quickly* so I could become a millionaire's wife in my lifetime. It never happened. Perhaps for him, nothing was the new something. What was his real ailment? *Newjobphobia, Jobseekerscitis or Lazylitus?*

He did not think about his aged dad *(well, he may have done, but not to my knowledge),* let alone helping his mother or his battalion of siblings. Occasionally, I did try to give them what little I could, but since I was the only one working and earning a living, I usually did not have much left after paying the bills and using the remainder for the upkeep of the house.

Every time I asked why he was not sending money home to support his family, his reply was always, 'I don't want to give them just anything like you do, I'll give them a lot when I hit the big time.' The saying *'a little is better than nothing'* did not exist in his world. It certainly baffled me how a person could change from one extreme to the other almost overnight.

★ ★ ★

One night, as I sat watching television in the living room, waiting for James to return home, I dozed off and was awoken by the sound of his key turning in the door. I stood up yawning, welcomed him and switched off the television, as I could hear the annoying, long, low *b-e-e-p* tone, which indicated that the TV station had finished their broadcast and was off the air.

As I headed to the kitchen to get his food, he informed me that he was not hungry, as he had already eaten while he was out. I had no idea what time it was, but I guessed it must have been after 1.00a.m. in the morning for the television station to have gone off the air. *I checked the clock on the wall. It was 3.14a.m.*

When he informed me he had already eaten and was not going to eat, I stopped dead in my tracks and turned to face him. I was fed up and infuriated. There were no apologies or remorse from him whatsoever and I could no longer bear or tolerate his nonsense, lack of consideration, concern or regard for me. I had to confront him.

'What on earth do you mean by that, James?'

'I mean what I have just said, my fair lady. I am not eating again!' He pronounced the words so emphatically they were like the strokes of a cane on my bare back.

I began to protest, 'But I went to the trouble of cooking a meal without...'

He simply brushed past me and made his way to the bedroom to undress. I followed him in with my words of grievance, watching him undo his shirt buttons after finishing my statement.

A few tense minutes passed by, as he skilfully evaded my eyes, while I tried to look straight into his eyeballs.

Furious, I asked him, 'Honey, why did you not care to inform me until now that you had already eaten? I would not have bothered cooking for you.' Still angry, I added, 'Also, why do you enjoy being away from home all the time? Do you hate me that much or do you have another family I don't know about?'

He never uttered a word or bothered to reply to any of my questions. Instead, when he had finished unbuttoning his shirt, he took it off and threw it on the bed, advancing towards me as if in slow motion. His jaw clenched and unclenched, his fists tightened and his twin pecs were dancing from side to side on the broad, bare chest I used to love caressing. Fear engulfed me and I became very scared of the *stranger-turned-Frankenjames* lunging towards me.

'Uh-oh', I said, and began to retrace my steps backwards.

'How dare you question me like that? Are you my Mother?' He roared as he got closer. It was as if I was watching a bad movie. He balled his right palm into a fist and aimed it at me.

'James, please don't!' I shouted at him, horror contorting my face. I attempted to run but I was immobilised with fear so I slipped and lost my balance. In my effort to get up and escape, he grabbed me, pinned me to his chest with his left arm and began punching away at me.

While he was getting all *Bruce Lee* on me, there was no chance of escaping from him. As I tried to wriggle out of his powerful grip in which I was locked, I realised he was stoned. I could smell the sickening stench of the mixture of booze and weed on his breath. He had handled his state of stupor well and seemed normal to me when he walked through the door. Even while taking his clothes off, I still did not notice. Had I known, I would never have dared to question him.

James then targeted my sides and carried on pounding away mercilessly. This man was going to kill me very soon, I thought. He must have been very intoxicated and unaware of the extent of the damage he could do or might already have done so far. By this time, I was already wailing and screaming, although I did not recognise the sound of my own voice. To me it sounded like someone else was crying outside the room.

It was almost 4.00a.m. in the morning. Everywhere was quiet and James, even in his condition, must have realised that someone might hear me screaming and call the police. This realisation, therefore, must have made him eventually come to his senses and he let go of me. Shocked and writhing in pain, I coiled up in the foetal position. I could not believe that James, who I loved so much, could have raised his littlest finger against me, let alone pounded me like that.

Breathing heavily, he stomped out to the balcony. I guess he went to check to see if anyone was around and had heard anything or to get some fresh air, or may be, to smoke some more. He came back inside after a few minutes, shut the door gently, and locked it behind him. I had since managed to pull myself from off the floor and onto the sofa. Seconds later, I sensed he was becoming remorseful. Hot tears were cascading down his cheeks as he snuggled up to me and started to console me on the two-seater sofa.

'What did I do to make you do that James?' I asked in a small voice.

He apologised for his behaviour, but blamed the devil, booze, wakibaki and me, for questioning and disrespecting him. He then swore he would never ever lay his hands on me again and promised to stop drinking and smoking.

Completely overwhelmed by the wave of emotion at the sight of his tears, I believed him. It was not his fault. I had made him angry by questioning him and he lost it. For that reason, I forgave him and we made up. There was no trace of blood on me, but there were bruises on my arms, sides and lower body. I looked and felt like I had been wrestling with a big cat but I did not go to the hospital for treatment, neither did I report his assault to the police nor to anyone else. Instead, I took some pain-relief tablets and went to bed, but I could not sleep.

Little did I know I was embarking on a journey that every battered woman dreads; a lonely life of misery!

After recovering from the initial shock and the painful memory that surfaced of him battering me, I took a good look at myself. I was a mess. My hands, sides, thighs and legs were bruised as though my body had been panel-beaten. I was *purple*. I felt sad, degraded, worthless, subdued, used and abused; feeling no less humiliated than I had been after the search by the female customs officer at Heathrow. The worst part, however, was the throbbing pain.

I tried to get up and out of bed in the morning but I could not, due to the pain. When I told James, he asked me to stay in bed, to *chill out and relax*. Then came the wonder of all wonders when he promised to make me some breakfast. That both shocked and surprised me since he had never cooked or done anything nice or romantic for me since our courtship days or honeymoon period. An hour later he got out of bed, gave me a peck on the cheek and headed straight for the kitchen.

Pondering while alone in the room, with my eyes roving around, scanning and taking everything in, my eyes finally settled on the white ceiling. Before long, I was gazing into space and I soon brushed the ill feelings away and disconnected from my grief. Denial set in again and confusion clouded my sense of clarity. I was thinking and believing that what James had done to me was normal in any marriage. After all, I had witnessed my Dad beat my Mum, Steppy and us, his children, too, on several occasions.

As a result, I began to reason and rationalise that what James had done was not unusual and so I should not be shocked. I also refused to believe that James would deliberately hurt me. Were it not for his drinking and smoking habits which clouded his judgment, he probably would not have done what he did.

I started to play the blame game in my head. I did not only blame myself for interrogating him when he came in at *beer o'clock,* I also foolishly and falsely believed that since he had never done this before, he would certainly not do it again because he loved me.

With the benefit of hindsight now, I know I was being narrow-minded and stupid. All I knew then was that I loved him and he loved me in his own way. I felt that as long as I did everything I could to please him, plead with him *(although he had promised, I prayed he meant it)* to give up smoking, encourage him to cut down on the boozing and the late nights, he would change for the better.

Perhaps, with our joint effort, we would be able to make our marriage work so we could be happy. Our marriage should be for better or worse. No relationship is perfect; they all have their difficulties, so why would our marriage be an exception or immune from conflicts?

★ ★ ★

James returned to the room carrying a tray containing a side plate with two slices of buttered toast and a plate of scrambled eggs. I managed to pull myself up into a sitting position against the headboard, then took the tray from him and balanced it on my lap. I thanked him for the food and for looking after me, with a little smile playing around my lips. It was clear I was enjoying every bit of the attention and despite the scrambled eggs being a bit too salty, I gave him 100% for making an effort and then wolfed it all down.

As I am not a tea or coffee drinker, I asked James for a glass of water so I could take some pain relieving tablets. While he went for it, I quickly asked him to bring me the cordless telephone so I could call my boss at work. I had to inform him I was under the weather *(or rather unbelievably, under James's care)*.

At least I got some solace in ordering and bossing him around a bit. After all, had he not beaten me up, I would have had to do these things myself, and since he had shown some remorse, there was no harm in making him clean up his mess.

After notifying my boss, I continued to lie in bed as James had instructed. He stayed with me and was at my beck and call all day long. *James, available and at home throughout the day without going out?* I could not believe it and almost begged him to beat me every day if that would keep him at home more.

In fact, knowing what I know now, I should have reported him to the police and pressed charges against him. More to the point, it would have been wise to divorce him, as I also know that for most men who batter their wives, it simply only takes the first time. *If he hits you once, he will hit you repeatedly, again, and...*

I really do believe now, from experience that the truest form of love is how you behave towards someone and not how you feel about him or her. A person's actions will tell you all you need to know!

★ ★ ★

Generally, after the battering, things changed slightly for the better, but he soon started staying out late again. He was always on the defensive when I asked about his whereabouts and this would invariably lead to fights. His promises about curbing his bad habits flew out of the window and he was constantly moody.

Whoever this man was, had a personality flaw, he was not my James; someone had replaced him. At times, no matter what I did or said, he still hit me, and at other times, regardless of how rude I was, it was as if he could not be bothered.

From then onwards, his mere existence led to my emotional devastation. His physical, verbal, emotional and mental abuse graduated to another level. *A higher one!*

I regularly ended up bruised and battered, as I never stood a chance against this karate black-belter who was exceptionally quicker with his fists and feet than *Speedy Gonzales*. I bore it all because I was blindly in love and I was foolish not to have thought or considered that his love for me may have been nothing but fake.

His behaviour made me doubt whether he had ever genuinely loved me or if he had truly found out about my British status from some of my friends, before I knew him and then had sprinted his way into my heart.

Was I his meal ticket to England? Was he living off me? It was becoming very difficult not to answer these questions in the affirmative. I was extremely sad that I had dropped some of my friends who were caring and bold enough to warn me about James when they began to recognise the warning signs.

Even if my suspicions were correct about him falling in love with my identity rather than with me, I could not prove it and even if I could, it was too late. After all, he had me hook, line and sinker. If I were a man, I would say he had me by the balls and it did not matter whether he was playing the game fairly.

The truth was that I was already married to him and despite these silly thoughts or assumptions, I was still deeply in love with him, hence my decision to carry on. I resigned myself to be the kind of wife who got slapped and stayed put. What I was suffering at the hands of James was the cross I had to bear and it was mine alone to carry.

★ ★ ★

Whenever we fought and he ended up beating me *(more precisely, while his papers were being processed and he was still on a one-year probationary period under immigration law),* several attempts made on my part to notify the police were hindered by him. He would kick the cordless telephone from out of my hands, *kung fu style,* then apologise and beg for my forgiveness until I gave in.

However, when he was granted indefinite leave to remain in the country, he would hand me the phone and say, 'Here, take it, call the police officers that are both your Father and Mother, you British bastard.' He also mocked and advised me to tattoo the letters BB on my forehead. His favourite name for me became *fool* after tactically dropping the *honey* he used to call me.

There is a parable my sweet Mother often refers to which is: *'If there is too much dirt in a bowl of soup, even a blind man will notice it.'* It was the most appropriate idiomatic expression about my relationship with James until that point. His behaviour, attitude and conduct were all so appalling that even I, who loved him very dearly, had begun to notice it. He had planted a seed of uncertainty and deceit, which was pregnant and growing by the day...

The tide had turned and everything had fallen apart. The real James was now apparent and the wool had been pulled from over my eyes. Amidst all of these events, I more or less believed that I really was a fool! Even so, I still did not condemn him totally. I often wallowed in the delusion that in some ways he may have retained some fondness for me. *Like*, but definitely not love, as I had previously deceived myself or had always assumed.

Besides, I often believed I was partly to blame for all the scuffles we were having. Due to my naivety, I was not wise enough to avoid him whenever he came home late and drunk. Instead, according to him, my *pestering* and *nagging* about his whereabouts angered him so much and this, therefore, gave him an excuse to beat me mercilessly upon his return.

I picked up a leaflet on Relate when I went to my GP's surgery for an appointment and it contained information about the Relate's services *(a relationship counselling service that improves relationships)*. Having read a couple of pages while waiting for my turn, I found it to be very informative and I wrote down the number discreetly in my diary in case I ever needed it.

When I got home, I hid it safely away from James in order to seek advice while he was out, but each time I dialled the number, I hung up as soon as the phone was answered. I was living in denial and had concluded that if I spoke to someone about my marital problems, the abuse would become real.

★ ★ ★

Due to societal expectations within the Nigerian culture and community, home or abroad, a woman is supposed to keep her house in order. Her home is her kingdom and she is the glue that holds her family together. Should anything go wrong, she is the first suspect.

This perception occasionally led me to believe I was a failure and I was beginning to doubt my sense of reasoning. I sincerely felt I had failed James somewhere down the line and was responsible for his misbehaviour. I often thought, that it may be what I had done or had left undone that had led to his drinking, smoking and habitual late nights. These were the many unreasonable excuses I made to justify his atrocious behaviour.

Growing up in a polygamous home, my dad had beaten us all up countless times and I thought that was normal life. Domestic violence is not a big deal in Nigeria. It is a common occurrence. For a man to decide to beat or discipline his wife in order to teach her a lesson is no *biggie,* as is often said in Nigeria. It is regularly considered the norm and widely acceptable there.

The truth is, whether you reside in Nigeria or not, and regardless of where you live within the Nigerian community abroad, wife beating is not perceived as abnormal. This is one of the reasons many women simply resign themselves to their fate and endure their marriages rather, than enjoy them.

The fear of my marriage ending up the way my parents' did, or being treated the way Dad had treated Mum was a constant worry for me. On the other hand, living in England reassured me a little, as polygamy is not acceptable. That notwithstanding, who was to say James would not dump me or go off with someone else anyway? After all, he was already in the UK, he had gotten what he wanted and he did not have to be *Evo-Stik* glued to me.

I wanted to give the best of me that I could so my marriage would work, but I was constrained! I internalized my situation and lived in constant fear; not daring to tell anyone what I was going through at the hands of James. To the world, he was my prince charming and at home, nothing but an incredible hulk. I had very few friends, but I hid it all from them and my family, as not many people would have believed me if my nightmarish situation ever got out.

Regardless of my personal feelings of fear, failure and shame, I also worried about the repercussions and people's perceptions of me. I was almost certain I would be solely to blame, scorned or sneered at because he was always so charming, sweet, respectful and pleasant to outsiders. No one would ever imagine he was capable of hurting even a fly.

★ ★ ★

I used to be a bubbly, outgoing person, but I soon became a shadow of my former self and gradually turned into an introvert with very low self-esteem. The qualities I possessed as a person before I met and married James had either faded, been squeezed out of me or were no longer there. I regularly returned home from work to an empty house. No friends, no James since he was never home; *it was just me, myself and Irene!* I ended up losing perspective on myself and my situation to the point that I did not recognise who I was or who I was becoming.

I felt both physically drained and mentally exhausted, knowing that no matter how capable I thought I was, I was never strong enough to break free from the toxic relationship, which, for the sake of love, I had allowed myself to be so consumed by.

One day, as I stood before the mirror I exclaimed, 'Oh, my goodness...' The gaunt figure in front of me was horrible - a permanently sad, tired face. *Eye bags? Crow's feet too! Lines and wrinkles? Where did they all come from? No wonder he avoided me. Come to granny, James, for you turned me into this!*

His lifestyle must have taken a toil on me. I was stressed out and overwhelmed with shame and embarrassment. I was at my lowest! Marriage should be for better or worse, but not taken for granted. I still could not tell anyone what I was going through, so I soldiered on, in an obviously fruitless bid to solder the cracks in my marriage. The state of it all was consistently deteriorating rather than improving and I regularly had to pay dearly for the cost of keeping it together in order to maintain a united front.

Thinking about it now, I ask myself, 'Why on earth did I have to feel ashamed? Why did I foolishly continue to blame myself for all the problems between James and I? How did James succeed in making me believe I was responsible for the problems he was causing? This is perhaps an area for psychologists to research – how or why women who are madly in love with wife-beaters are manipulated by these men into believing they are the problem.

★ ★ ★

Life, to an extent, is all about the choices we make. Everyone has the right to make a choice, however, they should be prepared to face the consequences of those choices without blaming anyone else.

James chose alcohol and substance abuse. They were his best friends, or rather, he was married to them. The simple fact is that since I did not advise him to buy, use, shove or force them down his throat or up his nose, he had no business taking out his anger or frustrations on me. He should be liable and the one feeling ashamed, not me, for he was the junkie as well as the ingrate, not the other way round! Equally, nothing justifies hitting or beating a fellow human being, no matter the provocation. *Yours truly was only just gradually waking up to the reality!*

★ ★ ★

One of James's friends, called Rume, offered to take us out for a meal one evening. At exactly 4.00p.m., which was the stipulated time, he turned up in front of our house *(probably only one of the few Nigerians I knew who always arrived on time)* with his girlfriend, Natalie. It was a known fact that Rume had numerous girlfriends, but I only knew two of them, Phe, a Nigerian girl from London and Natalie, Welsh, from Cardiff. I thought Phe was joining us since she lived locally, but it was a nice surprise to see Natalie as I didn't know she was in town and I had not seen her in a while.

We set off after we had exchanged pleasantries and a few minutes later, Rume's mobile phone started to ring. He could not answer it since he was driving, but as soon as he noticed the caller's name was flashing as Phe, he quickly passed the phone over to James, to prevent Natalie from finding out who it was.

James was sitting in the back with me and he handled the matter like the deft and adept two-timer he is. He immediately had perfect knowledge of what was happening, answered the phone, but simply pretended he could not hear Phe very well.

'Hello, hello, I can't hear you', he said, waving the phone round and round in circles.

'Who is this? I can't hear you', James repeated, as he continued to move the phone in his hand from side to side, up and down and then blowing air into it with his mouth, pretending there was no reception.

'Hello, hello?' James continued, before hanging up. I smiled at him but said nothing. He had revealed and demonstrated his actions right before my very eyes; precisely the same way he had treated my calls the numerous times I had tried to contact him and could not reach him. He must have forgotten I was there and God had made him carelessly expose his dubious act to me. *Birds of a feather flock together...*

Natalie, sitting in front with Rume was oblivious to the matter, and although I felt sorry for her, I felt more sorry for myself. James never clicked that I had caught him in the act and at his game, he just carried on chatting to Rume, nonchalantly.

Rume drove us to a lovely African restaurant in Woolwich, South East London. The place was crowded with people laughing, eating, drinking and chatting. We were allocated a table on arrival and we sat down to order our food and drinks. I ordered my favourite dish of *jollof* rice, stockfish and *dodo* with a glass of white wine. Natalie had a plate of fried rice and beef with a glass of red wine. James and Rume each had a plate of pounded yam with *egusi* soup, assorted meats and two bottles of *Guilder* each *(a pale lager made by Nigerian Breweries PLC)*.

The food was excellent. We had a good time that evening as we chatted, told funny jokes and laughed. Never a dull moment with Rume; as an Urhobo man a.k.a.*Warri guy* from the Delta part of Nigeria, he certainly made our ribs *crack* from laughter.

Natalie drove us back home since Rume and James had more than just the two bottles of lager they each ordered initially. We got home after 10.30p.m. and although James was a little too merry, he later calmed down and there was no trouble.

We both went to bed after we had washed and he fell asleep while we reflected on how the evening had gone.

I'd had such a good time and was grateful to have been invited along. I did not want to spoil things by bringing up the mobile phone palaver, as that would not stop him from continuing to use the trick on me but the night would have ended woefully.

It was a surprise that I had been asked to join them and it was the first time I had ever been out with his friends. Well, I thought, there's always a first and it would be the first of many, I hoped. Perchance God had answered my prayers and things were beginning to look up and get better for me. Maybe James had finally realised how much he had wronged me and was trying to make up for it, or so I thought, as I fell asleep, happy and smiling...

The next day James went out and did not return until after 4.30a.m. I had dreamt too soon. My jubilation became short-lived and only existed in my dream. *Can a leopard change its spots?*

Rume visited us from time to time and because he liked food and I cooked well, he sometimes ate with us and *cracked our ribs* in return. Amazingly, that was the first, last and only time I was ever invited out with James's friends, to be precise; *friend*. Well, I have my good memories.

A few weeks later, James mentioned that Rume had been incarcerated in HMP Belmarsh Prison, Woolwich.

'Why? What was his offence?' I asked James.

'I don't know.' James answered blatantly. *Silly me, did I really believe he would furnish me with the details?*

Since they both led similar and irresponsible lifestyles, only God knew what Rume's offence was. Therefore, with his partner-in-crime banged up, perhaps it was a warning sign for them to part ways and time for James to change his habits. *Regardless of Rume's jokes, I secretly prayed that tweedledee and tweedledum would be tweedledone. For good!*

Chapter Thirteen:
Time To Act

It was a Thursday and my day off work. James had gone out as usual and I was bored and fed up. The weather was sunny outside so I decided to take a stroll in the park. I needed time to clear my head, to reflect on my relationship with James and to make sense of my situation and experiences. It was time for a reality check!

On arriving there, I scanned the area, found an empty spot and sat down on a bench. I began observing people as they were doing various things. There were several children playing happily with their parents or peers. Close by were quite a few couples affectionately holding hands, kissing or just chatting. Further ahead, I sighted a couple of singles too and I could not help but smile because I liked what I saw; a *happy picture* and I was glad for them all.

Thinking long and hard, I realised that the emotional, mental and physical abuse I was receiving from James, was not what I had bargained for. My feelings of guilt, fear, regret and anger were not just directed at him, but also at myself for having put up with it all for so long.

I had endured it because I loved him too much, but now I needed to take responsibility. I had to face reality by thinking with my head, so I refused to let my heart rule my head.

In doing so, I came up with the questions I truly needed to ask myself. 'Does love hurt? If it does not, why was I being punished for it? Also, why am I all torn up and excruciatingly crushed to the extent that my heart bleeds? Why was I so gullible to have suffered the abuse for so long? Marriage is hard graft, I knew that, but not to the point that it would be detrimental to my life. More importantly, why had I still allowed myself to go through it all, up until now? What should I do about the problem at this point? I needed answers and had to find a way forward.

Whilst pondering, I had an epiphany moment and every confusing thought seemed to click into place like the pieces of a puzzle. Suddenly, everything became clear and started to make sense. The truth *finally* dawned on me. It was true that I loved James, but I owed it to myself to love me first and much more. If James truly loved me, he would not put me through such heartache, let alone hit me.

Instantly, I got fed up with all his abuse; the tears of frustration, helplessness, of being mocked and ridiculed, of making numerous excuses for constantly having facial bruises and black eyes, and for having to wear dark sunglasses to cover them up in the middle of winter. In a nutshell, I was tired of papering over the cracks.

I decided enough was enough. I did not have to take his beatings anymore. As a result, I made a vow to myself that the next time James laid a finger on me, I would have to do something about it. I no longer wanted to continue walking on eggshells, predicting his mood swings or sitting like a lame duck waiting for the next attack. I realised I loved myself enough to take action before I ended up in the morgue.

★ ★ ★

A few weeks later, James and I were in the living room, chatting and sharing jokes after dinner, while the sound of Gregory Isaac's *Stranger in Town* was playing softly in the background. I was glad because he came home by about 8.00p.m. that day *(which was early for James)*. I was in stitches laughing at his funny jokes and at the way he was telling them, until the jokes turned into gibes, which gradually became offensive and ceased to amuse me any further.

One of James's gibes was, 'You do not have to beat your wife, partner or dog every day but you just have to make them think or believe that you will!' He then slapped the air to demonstrate what he meant and to drive home his point.

I stopped laughing as soon as I realised some of the gibes were indirectly targeted at me. When I pointed that out to him by asking what he meant by them, he said he was only joking. He then stopped, but only after calling me a spoilsport. Soon after, he began telling me how a friend of his had nearly assaulted a bus driver because the driver was rude and had spoken to his friend in a nasty way. James said he was unhappy about it and was tempted to join his friend to teach the arrogant driver a lesson.

I shook my head in disapproval and said I was glad he had not, as both he and his friend would have been in trouble or even sent to jail for assault. He looked at me as if I was a coward and said, 'Jail? Why, in God's name, would I be sent to jail for standing up for something I believe in? The man was a rude racist and ought to have been taught a lesson.'

'Not by you love', I said.

He was beginning to flare up as he continued. 'This is why the whole world is going mad. Everyone is scared to speak up when someone disrespects or oppresses you. This country is f★★★★d up!' He added, as I tried to reason with him by telling him that the best thing would have been to report the bus driver, not to have considered taking the law into his own hands.

I reminded him that it was an offence to assault any person working for the government, or anyone else, for that matter, but he would not listen and we started to argue as I tried to put my point across.

He shot a quick glance at me and said, 'How dare you argue with me, were you there? I said the stupid man was a complete racist.'

I ignored his look but told him to steer clear next time, unless he wanted to end up in serious trouble *(or even in jail, with his friend, Rume, I was tempted to say, but I knew better)*.

He was not happy that I was trying to tell him what to do and he tried to put me down as usual, saying, 'What do you know?' He looked at me with so much contempt that his eyes seemed to throw daggers my way.

He continued. 'Is it your wish for me to be as quiet as a mouse and to let people walk all over me? No way will I let that happen!'

I stared at him with my mouth wide open, gobsmacked that he had blown such a trivial matter out of proportion.

'You think you know everything', he carried on, 'but here's news for you, woman, you know nothing. A big fat nothing!' Stopping to catch his breath, I knew he was not finished with me yet. I was flabbergasted and I stood there with my mouth still agape, listening to his insults. I was fuming.

Seconds later, he added, 'When I want your opinion, I'll dial rent-an-idiot and during intelligent conversations, keep your mouth shut otherwise you will only end up proving how stupid you really are. Fool!'

Yes sir. That was me told. A tongue has no bones, but it can break one's heart. Mine broke instantly!

Brawling is not exactly my forte, but I felt so disgusted and angry at the way he had spoken down at me. I let out a small sigh, laughed, shook my head and said, 'James, you know what, it takes a fool to know one, which makes you a bigger fool than I am!'

I meant to add that he was the head of 'Mumu' progressive union, Uncle Way (for wayward), the chairperson of dunces (dundi united) and that his middle name must be Mugu. James, a.k.a. a man called Mugu (these are Naija's greatest titles for idiots (Mandiots), but I dared not breathe them out loud, as Mr. Mugu would have killed me instantly).

On hearing my short, but brave speech, he came charging at me, screaming and shouting like a bull that had just seen a red flag.

'Are you calling me a fool? Are you? Do I look like one to you?' Fire was burning in his eyes as he asked me the rhetorical questions. *Was Mr. Mugu expecting me to answer them? I knew better!*

I guess the combination of weed and booze must have stimulated his *waki-booze-baki-infested* brain to release a rush of endorphins and I could literally see the juices of anger begin to flow through his body.

'Oh no!' I said as I panicked and headed for the door. My heart was racing a mile a minute.

Being a sprinter, he moved very quickly and in a flash, just like a lion going for its prey, he grabbed me by the neck, almost choking me as I dropped on my knees, coughing and gasping for air. He then let go of my neck and dragged *tiny* me across the living room, punching me indiscriminately until I was crumpled on the floor. He went down with me.

The beating continued. I tried to shield my face with my hands, but that did not help. Instead, more punches landed on my face as I raised my head in an attempt to beg him to stop. He did not. I could barely see a thing and I was beginning to feel faint. My eyes were bloodshot, causing blurred vision. *(Holy Moses, is this how I am going to die, and at the hands of Mr. Mugu?)* I shuddered as the thoughts flashed through my mind.

This was no joke; James would not stop until he had killed me. I could not fight back but I blindly tried to push him away from me and screamed as loudly as I could so the neighbours or anyone would come to my rescue. *Wrong move!*

As I screamed, he struck me extremely hard across the face in so much of a blind fury that he almost knocked me into the next century. Then, he tried to put his filthy hands over my mouth to stop me from screaming. Totally pointless that was, as the slap had already done the trick.

With his one hand holding me down, I tried to bite a chunk out of the other grubby hand that was covering my mouth, but I could not even do that right. Instead, he became angrier that I had attempted or dared to bite him and he resumed punching me again, as if I was a punch bag.

At one point, I began to get punch-drunk and I was going weak. I was unsure if anyone had heard me screaming, but no one came to my rescue. After what seemed like an eternity or perhaps when he had got tired of punching me, he suddenly stopped. It was as though he had received an *(okay, that's enough),* order from his god of weed, and like a robot, he walked straight to our bedroom.

'Would it be an exaggeration for me to state that James acted like someone who was on drugs? What was wakibaki, weed or marijuana combined with booze classified as?' Hmm, I mused, *despite my condition.*

I could not move. I lay on the floor, motionless, as it still felt like he was punching me long after he had stopped. The pounding pain was unbearable; it felt like a massive truck had hit me. The world was whirling and swirling and I could see a thousand stars in my dazed state. I thought I was going to die.

A thought flashed through my semi-conscious mind as I struggled into a sitting position. Then dragging my legs painfully round under me across the living room floor, I knew I had to make it, though it seemed like forever. Finally I got there. I tried to stand, but I could not.

Using mind over matter, it took the last of my strength to stretch out in order to reach for the telephone receiver. With trembling hands, I felt for the numbers as I could barely see a thing through my bloodshot eyes. I was glad to hear the operator say, '999, which emergency services do you require please?'

★ ★ ★

After a few minutes of communication, I replaced the handset. I was happy and felt triumphant. I had done it. I had eventually summoned up enough courage to call the police and I was very proud of myself. *I might be a fool, but not that much of a bloody fool after all!*

Within the hour, there was a knock on our front door and when James came out of the bedroom to see who it was, he was surprised to see two police officers standing outside. All the same, he opened the door to let them in.

By that time, I had already managed to scrape myself from off the floor and onto one of the sofas in the living room. I did not want to go into the bedroom with James in there.

James eventually admitted to assaulting me and one of the officers arrested him, read him his rights and led him outside into the police car. The other officer stayed behind to radio a request for two female police officers who arrived within minutes. Afterwards, the first two officers drove off in the car with James.

I was a mess. A sorry sight! Seeing the state I was in, the female officers were very sympathetic, and as I began to narrate what had happened, I started to cry. One of the officers tried to console me, while the other took down my statement. I was asked if I wanted to see a doctor and although I was looking at them with a bruised face and swollen, puffy eyes, I assured them I was fine.

The *consoling* police officer advised that I had a choice and I could put a stop to being a victim of domestic violence. Next, I was informed of my rights and asked whether I was willing to press charges or not. I listened very carefully and after careful consideration, I made up my mind to press charges. They were glad to hear it and promised they would be back to take photographs of my bruises since they had not come with a camera.

However, when the two female police officers returned much later, I had changed my mind. I refused to press charges or to pursue the case any further. The *consoling* officer who had kind-heartedly advised me earlier was so shocked to learn that I had changed my mind, that one would think I was her sister.

She was very disappointed and did not hesitate to inform me that the next time James decided to do *his thing,* I might not even live long enough to call the police. I did not listen, after all, she was not my sister or a relative. I wanted to be left alone in my ignorance. I still loved James and was not prepared to let him go to jail, no matter what he did.

James had battered my self-confidence. My whole sense of reasoning flew out of the window. My epiphany or whatever moment I thought I had had, went down the drain. My brain and train of thought derailed. All I could think of was James and I prayed he would not suffer while in police custody. The other officer informed me she was ready to take the photos and after a few shots, they left.

★ ★ ★

After a little while, my sense of reasoning flew back in and I was able to think a bit rationally. I assumed that staying overnight in a police cell must have shaken James to his very core. Perhaps the spare time had enabled him to reflect on his life and made him reminisce about the good times. Also, I prayed that it had knocked some sense into him and had taught him an invaluable lesson or two.

He was released the next day and returned home like a dog with its tail between its legs. Since I had refused to press any charges against James, he was not taken to court. He was only arrested, detained overnight and set free the following day. By law, that was all the authorities were allowed to do in those days. Their hands were tied unless I pressed charges.

He was very remorseful as he begged for my forgiveness and he almost cried me a *river*. Flooded with sympathy, I told him I had forgiven him the very moment he left in the police car, but he must swear never ever to hit me again. He did.

He looked rough, dishevelled and dirty from being in the police cell, while I still felt bruised, battered and unclean, despite having taken a painful shower after the assault.

We therefore decided to take a shower together and it felt like the good old days had returned once again. As he slowly undressed me, he noticed my bruises and he was so sorry that he wept again. I reassured him that they were not as bad as they seemed and no longer hurt that much, which made him feel a bit better. He was very gentle with me and our shower together lasted almost an hour. We stood under the shower, lathered ourselves repeatedly with soap, and kissed each other lovingly; it felt so amazing and I enjoyed every minute of it.

After a while, we proceeded to scrub our bodies until we were squeaky clean. From the shower, he scooped my slender body into his strong loving arms. His eyes glued to mine as he carried me into our bedroom where we crawled under the sheets for a hot, passionate make out session. Completely satiated, we held each other, softly caressing our spent bodies until we fell asleep.

We had another shower when we woke up, got dressed and then I put on my *(guess who had just been battered)* dark sunglasses to hide my bruises. Thereafter, we went to a nearby African restaurant for a mouth-watering meal of fried rice, fresh fish stew and fried plantains *dodo*. My mouth hurt a little while eating, but it was well worth it. Making up was heavenly! *'The best bit about falling out, is making up.'* I thought, smiling sheepishly to myself.

★ ★ ★

The new James went with the police officers, and I got my old James back, the one I fell in love with. I found it hard to believe that it took a night in a police cell for James to realise, value and treasure what we had. He later made considerable effort to curb his wayward lifestyle by reducing his daily smoking and alcohol consumption.

There was a noticeable difference in his temper, attitude and behaviour, which were now a little more controlled. He limited his frequent outings and often returned home earlier. I was very happy and silently prayed and hoped to God that the monster in him never surfaced again.

We were both glad when I became pregnant in December 1992 and things were okay for a while. It did not last long though, as James soon reverted to his old paranoid self. He must have forgotten his trip to the police cell, as he consistently went to town on me; sometimes beating me to a pulp, regardless. In anger one night, he hit me so hard on my belly after an argument that I thought I had lost my baby. Miraculously, I did not. Thank God. I never reported the incident because he begged and consoled me *again*.

On Saturday, June 5 1993, I was six months pregnant. James went out as normal and did not return home, even though it was very late. After many futile attempts to contact him, I fell asleep but woke up just before 5.00a.m. to find his side of the bed still empty. My heart began to ache and I started to panic, thinking he had been involved in an accident or he had been mugged. I wore my winter coat over my nightgown and went outside, all alone; not caring about my own safety in the early hours of the morning.

The weather was very breezy and chilly for a summer morning and my breath hung thickly in the cold air; my legs trembling. Yet, all I could think of was James. Where was he? I felt sick both in my heart and in my stomach as I waited outside for about four and a half hours.

James finally strolled along, nonchalantly at about 9.40a.m. as high as a kite. He was a little startled when he saw me waiting outside but said nothing. Instead, he pushed the door open with his right foot, went in and headed straight for the bedroom without any explanation or remorse.

I followed behind and reminded him that I had been waiting òutside for him *(just in case he was too out of it to remember. It was a miracle he had got home safely)*. He slumped onto the bed and his reply, after only raising his head slightly from the pillow to answer me was, 'Do you want a medal? Hmm. I never asked you to', and with that, his head dropped back on the pillow like he was dead. He dozed off as soon as his head hit the pillow and he hadn't even taken off his clothes or shoes.

I took off his shoes, crawled into bed next to him and waited for him to sleep it off. I had learnt from experience that arguing with a *stoned junkie* James was useless and only led to nothing but quarrels. Therefore, I left him to sleep until he returned to the land of the living, when he would be sober enough to explain his whereabouts. I was exhausted too and I dozed off soon after.

Chapter Fourteen:
A Close Shave

F ive days later, on Thursday, June 10, I strolled to get some groceries from a nearby Co-op supermarket. It was a beautiful summer afternoon and the supermarket was only a two-minute walk from my home. On arriving there, I picked up an empty shopping basket, but dropped it a few minutes later without putting a single item in it. I felt a trickle of water running down my legs. At first I thought it was sweat, but became panicky when I looked down and saw a puddle of water on the floor, which had flowed from between my thighs.

I ran home as quickly as my legs could carry me. Fortunately, James was at home ironing his shirt, although he was getting ready to go out. When I told him what had happened, he immediately rang our GP's surgery and he was told to dial 999, because my waters had broken and I was in labour.

999? Waters broken. Labour? How could this be happening at 26 weeks rather than at 40 weeks? It was not even time for my first antenatal appointment. My due date was in September, my birthday month. I was expecting to have a Virgo baby. It was too early and I had not bought a single item for my baby. All I'd had was my first scan. A million thoughts ran through my mind.

I was hysterical. I could not believe what was happening. I felt as if I was in a trance and before I could pull myself together, the ambulance had pulled up in front of Guy's Hospital, London Bridge. Quickly, but gently, I was lowered into a wheelchair and wheeled straight into the labour ward.

I asked the doctor what had caused my waters to break so early and he said it could have been due to the weather, stress or another unidentifiable reason. My mind flashed back to the cold early hours of Sunday morning breeze I had exposed myself to while waiting for James. Could that have caused it? Perhaps it was the blow he dealt me in the belly previously or was it stress?

True, I had been under a lot of stress due to James's irresponsible behaviour. If there was any possibility of them all being linked, I concluded that James had succeeded in destroying my baby and I. In addition to the above mentioned, I blamed myself for foolishly allowing my worries to affect my poor baby.

The doctor explained the practical details to us and stated that there was a high risk of brain haemorrhage or brain damage in pre-term babies. As a result, I would have to be given a corticosteroid injection to help my baby's lungs develop faster, as well as to boost its chances of survival.

The survival rate for premature babies born that early at the time was only 30/70, 19 years ago now.[1]

I had the injection and I was later taken to one of the wards to rest. After dinner, I was very eager to know more about my situation so I struck up a conversation with a nurse in order to pick her brains *(and by Jove, did I pick the right one)*. She told me that the amniotic fluid, which normally surrounds and protects babies, can completely leak out of the vagina. She further explained that the amniotic sac prevents germs from getting into the uterus and the amniotic fluid, but if the uterus becomes infected, the baby may have to be delivered immediately.

I was sure she had only just graduated from the School of Midwifery and had crammed all of these words into her brain in order to pass her exams. Most of the things she said might as well have been Greek to me, but

---

[1]Mail Online (also known as dailymail.co.uk) http://www.dailymail.co.uk/femail/article-93556/Premature births.html Thursday, 17 May 2012 on premature births states the following facts:
'The UK has the highest rate of premature births in Europe. Approximately one in eight babies born in the UK every year is born prematurely or becomes ill soon afterwards. Out of these 70,000 babies, around 18,000 need intensive care.'
'The good news is survival rates for premature babies have increased in the last 20 years. Nearly 80% of babies weighing 2lb 2oz, or "sugar bag babies" as they are sometimes known as are now expected to live compared to 20% in 1980.'
'The good news is that babies born at 23 weeks have a 17% chance of survival, those born at 24 weeks have a 39% chance and babies born at 25 weeks have a 50% chance of survival.'
'Some famous premature babies include Albert Einstein, Sir Winston Churchill and Stevie Wonder; so there are exceptions to every rule.'

I narrowed it down to water leakage, infection and may give birth immediately.

She advised me not to use any form of sanitary towels to prevent any blockages, but to persevere, since my baby was better in the womb rather than out; while the water was dripping and still only in trickles. Finally, she warned that I might go into labour at any moment.

Much later, I did some research and found out that a number of factors can contribute to premature births. I could only relate to what had happened to me, as shown below:

Low socio-economic status:

(a) 'There appears to be an association between high levels of stress, particularly chronic stress and preterm birth. The theory is that severe stress can lead to the release of hormones that can trigger uterine contractions and preterm labour.'

(b) 'This may explain why women who are victims of domestic abuse have a higher risk for spontaneous preterm labour. Those who endure physical violence have an even greater risk, of course, particularly if there's trauma to the abdomen.' Expert advice from BabyCenter.

★ ★ ★

I stayed in the hospital and prayed fervently for God to allow my pregnancy to reach at least seven months, as there was more chance of my baby surviving then. I also learnt that Guy's Hospital was the best place to be in, being a specialist hospital for premature babies. That piece of information reassured me greatly and I left the rest in God's hands.

By midday, on Wednesday June 16, I began to experience some discomfort in my stomach that felt more like period pains or cramps. I believed this was normal with pregnancy and thought nothing of it because it was bearable, until it got worse by the hour.

I notified a nurse who held onto my wrist as if she was checking for my pulse. She asked me to squeeze her wrist each time I felt the pain, which I did with my left hand. After timing the intervals at which I squeezed her wrist, she told me that I was having contractions, but I was not ready to deliver the baby yet. 'Contractions?' I exclaimed, 'Oh my God, does this mean I have to begin to prepare for labour?' The nurse simply smiled as she left, but promised to check on me again.

When she returned much later, I was in so much agony that after timing the frequency of my contractions, the time between one contraction and another grew less and less. It meant the baby was close, so the nurse immediately arranged for my transfer to the labour ward.

On arriving there, I asked one of the nurses on the labour ward if she could kindly help me contact James to inform him that I had moved wards. She seemed very nice and she agreed. After thanking her, I gave her the numbers for both his mobile phone and our landline, which she called several times, but there was no response.

I started to panic. I needed James with me, as there was a possibility I would be delivering our baby any time that day. *Where was James?* I did not want him to miss the birth of our first child!

Unfortunately, all efforts to reach James proved futile. An hour later, one of my friends called Bose visited me and I asked her to stay with me in case anything happened to me. James was not available, so if there was any need for her to sign on my behalf, I told her she would have to do it. It was a huge responsibility, although, she had no choice but to agree.

As if the pain I was experiencing was not agonising enough, a nurse inserted a syntocinon drip into my arm to induce stronger contractions. The reason, the nurse explained, was because the foetus was too small and would need extra help with being pushed out of the uterus and into the birth canal.

Chapter Fifteen:
My Greatest Gift On Earth!

The pains caused by the drip were intense. The contractions came quicker, got stronger and it became unbearable. It was getting very late. The lovely nurse still could not reach James, but she kept trying to phone him nevertheless. The fact that James was not there to comfort or stand by me did not help. This was his first child; it was only fair for him to be with me and to support me through the process. I was scared.

It was my first time and the baby was very early. *Scary!* The thought of James not being there only added to my pain and I felt dizzy from using the gas and air, which gave me nothing but nausea. I had no relief whatsoever. I was totally distressed and in agony.

I had read about an epidural injection in a mother and baby magazine a few weeks before and it had to be the remedy for my torture. Although it stated there were some side effects, I was not bothered as I intended to worry about that later. For now, anything was better than this pain, so I requested an ESI *(Epidural Steroid Injection)*.

A doctor injected the ESI drug around my spinal cord and like magic, my pain disappeared a few minutes afterwards. I could not believe I was no longer in pain. All I could see was a graph showing my contractions going up and down as I watched it on the screen of the monitor. *'Why had I not requested it until now? Anyway, better late than never!'* I thought. Thank God for epidurals. *God bless the inventors.* I would recommend it to anyone.

James arrived some minutes past midnight and explained that he had gone to get me some food. Food? What food? Where was it? I was not hungry or bothered about food, but hungry for James to arrive and I was ecstatic he was not going to not miss the birth of his first child.

Amidst my happiness, I forgot my pain, by which time the epidural had worn off, just in time for me to push. I had the zeal to go on and to push harder with James's words of encouragement *(although, I nearly broke the whole of his ten bastard fingers when the pain hit me hard)*. After the final push, at exactly 1.06 am., I had my baby, a boy, our son. As soon as I saw him, a name immediately sprang to my lips. JAMIE! Welcome.

Strangely enough, all throughout my pregnancy, I frequently thought about baby names, but could not come up with a single one I liked for either a boy or girl. The name Jamie never once crossed my mind and it is funny how it appeared the moment he entered the world.

Exactly what I had prayed for came precisely one week later, as God had answered my prayers. I arrived at the hospital on a Thursday and the following Thursday, the 17th of June, was the very day I entered my 7th month of pregnancy. It was also my 27th week. Jamie was born 13 weeks early and had survived. Great is Thy faithfulness, Oh Lord!

Jamie was so tiny. He weighed approximately two pounds (1100g), the equivalent of a bag of sugar. There was barely any skin to cover his bones as it looked virtually transparent and almost visible to the human eye. I could see his lungs pumping away and his breathing was very fast because he was fighting to survive against the odds. In that instant I knew Jamie was a fighter; my little hero. I hoped!

Initially, the doctor and nurses attached the necessary ventilators and monitors to Jamie as precautionary measures, before rushing him to the Special Care Baby Unit *(SCBU)*. Unbelievably, just before Jamie was taken away, he stretched out his little arm, then he opened and closed his tiny palm as if to say, *'See you soon, Mum!'* That was the sign I needed from God to reassure me that Jamie would be fine and I was overwhelmed with joy.

Thankfully, there were no complications on my side either. Within minutes, one of the nurses wheeled me in a wheelchair to have a shower. I felt strong enough to stand up and wash myself, and in less than thirty minutes, James and I were with our son in the SCBU.

The very sight of Jamie in the incubator with all the monitors attached to him, still fighting to stay alive brought fresh tears to my eyes. I wanted to stay and watch Jamie all night, but the nurses reminded me that I had only just given birth and advised me to go and rest since they would be watching him.

I was given a private room, rather than being put on a ward full of mums who had recently given birth, but had their babies by their side. As I walked through the wards, I became very emotional and as soon as I got to my room, I broke down and sobbed hysterically.

'Why are you crying? Do you doubt God? You should be thanking Him for keeping Jamie alive instead of crying.' James said as he tried to console me.

What he said made absolute sense. James himself must be relying on God to help Jamie and if he had any worries or doubts at all, he never showed them. He spent the night with me and together we cuddled up on the single hospital bed. It did not bother me that the bed was too small for both of us, I was just glad James was there with me and I slept peacefully after we had prayed. The thought that God would see Jamie through gave me hope throughout the night.

In the morning, James was still by my side when I woke up. I looked at his handsome face, he was sleeping like a baby and snoring softly. It felt like the good times again. My James! Perhaps becoming a dad had had something to do with his newfound sense of responsibility. I prayed silently that it would last forever as I got up quietly to take a shower to avoid disturbing him. Shortly after, James woke up, smartened himself up and together we went down to see our son.

On arriving there, we were surprised to see that most of the ventilators had been taken off Jamie. They were no longer necessary as he was breathing and coping well without the supporting gadgets. Super-strong guy, my Jamie! The only problem was that he was still very tiny, but there were no complications and his health was perfect.

★ ★ ★

Certified fit, well and discharged after ten days, I left the hospital, but visited Jamie twice daily. He had jaundice a few times, but he was fully cured on each occasion and after six weeks in the hospital, Jamie was well and ready for home. At that point, he weighed four pounds and ten ounces. To me, and compared to what he had weighed when he was born, he was big.

Prior to his discharge, James and I went shopping, in order to get ready for Jamie's arrival. We bought most of the things we needed, such as his baby cot and other essentials, since we had not bought anything previously. I spent Jamie's last night at the hospital with him to attend a short CPR *(cardiopulmonary resuscitation)* first-aid course in case there were any eventualities when we got home. That same night, I bought gifts and cards for the wonderful staff on Jamie's ward to show our appreciation and I intend to fulfil my promise by taking Jamie back there someday.

James picked me up from the hospital the next morning to return later in the afternoon with Mum and Max. They accompanied us to the hospital to take Jamie home, while the rest of the family *(including Government)* waited at home for the homecoming party. My sister Christine bought all his first cute clothes and nappies; especially for premature babies, and most of our friends and families brought him gifts too.

Taking Jamie home was one of the happiest days of my life. He settled in perfectly, but caught bronchitis when he was three months old. It was a very trying period for me financially, emotionally and physically. I was on income support as I had had to give up work to look after Jamie full-time.

At first, James was very helpful, but as time went by, he relapsed into his old habits and the devil in him resurfaced again. I became more or less like a single parent since he was hardly ever at home; leaving me to care for a young premature baby all by myself. When he was at home, the slightest argument would set him off, whether he was under the influence of narcotics or not. Frankly, I must admit now that sometimes it was safer and healthier *(for me)* for him to be out.

★ ★ ★

My mum became a businesswoman after all my siblings arrived from Nigeria, just before our wedding. As a result, she was always in and out of the UK or buying goods from all over the world to sell in Nigeria, but she helped me greatly each time she visited us. Auntie Pat, on the other hand, was always at the end of the telephone and she never failed to remind me that Jamie was a fighter.

There were numerous times I called out the ambulance service while Jamie was ill. All alone with a very young child, I often had no money for a taxi on leaving the hospital *(there were usually no buses after midnight or in the early hours of the morning)*. James had our car, but he was hardly ever at home and I could never reach him. As a result, I sometimes had no choice but to contact some of his friends, who forever claimed they had no knowledge of his whereabouts.

On one occasion, Tony, one of his closest friends, kindly offered to pick us up from the hospital in the early hours of the morning. He was so disgusted with James's behaviour after taking us home, that he decided to stay with us and waited to scold him on his return.

James returned home after 4.00a.m. and was surprised to see his friend Tony. When James asked what he was doing in his house, Tony explained how he had picked us up from the hospital because we were stranded. To that, James only mumbled a lousy *thanks* and never even looked at Jamie or asked if he was ok. Instead, he went straight to bed and Tony left in anger.

I had already had enough, but could do nothing about it. *I concluded long ago that he had a stubborn streak a mile wide.* With just having had a new baby, I needed to reserve my energy to look after Jamie and to perform my wifely duties. I had no zeal to fight anymore.

Thank God, Jamie was getting better. James apologised in the morning and I forgave him after his promises for the umpteenth time that he would change, which he did, but as expected, only for a short while. *Is it too early or late to say at this stage that he was already sounding like a broken record?*

★ ★ ★

Months later, James returned home earlier than usual one evening and asked me to get myself and Jamie ready. To my surprise he wanted to treat us to dinner at the Planet Hollywood Restaurant in the West End of

London. I was very excited, since it was one of the latest restaurants in town and I was hoping to catch a glimpse of one or all of the Hollywood mega-star owners, namely Sylvester Stallone, Bruce Willis, Arnold Schwarzenegger and Demi Moore.

On arriving there, the place was packed full with people of all age groups and there were many others waiting to get in. James, unfortunately, had not made a table reservation in advance and we had to wait outside for a couple of hours.

Despite the long wait, we were hit with all the *ables*. Sadly, we were neither *able* to get in, nor *capable* of eating there without a booked *table*. *Worst still, we were unable* to see any of the owners from Hollywood *(let alone to dine with the stars)*. However, the friendly members of staff constantly acknowledged us and promised to inform us of any cancellations.

We eventually gave up waiting and wandered around the restaurant to check out some of the original film memorabilia, which were great to see in real life. When James spotted some lovely souvenirs, he promised to buy them for us and although I told him not to worry, he insisted. He was in a good mood, we were all happy and I thanked him for his kind intentions, which he acknowledged. James did not bother to enlighten me about how or from where he had got the money and I did not ask either. I did not dare.

At the merchandise shop, he bought me a lovely pink Planet Hollywood T-shirt, for Jamie, a cute powder blue Planet Hollywood hat and a black baseball cap for himself. After touring on empty stomachs without any hope of getting in, we were starving. So we headed for the nearest McDonald's and settled for Big Mac meals instead.

Planet Hollywood did not work out for us as planned, but we had left the house, went out together as a family and we made a good evening out of it. I thanked James again for making the effort and even if we never got to eat in the restaurant as he had initially intended, he had done well in terms of *it's the thought that counts.*

Chapter Sixteen:
Old Dog, New Tricks

J ames and I were okay, or so I thought, even though we still had our fair share of difficulties. On a rare evening when he had come home about 7.00p.m or 8.00p.m., we sat down together as a family to watch an African movie. It was about a woman who was struggling to make ends meet while her husband was in jail. Her husband's best friend came to her rescue and helped her, but he also could not help falling in love with her, while her husband was still locked up.

James's paranoia led him to turn fiction into reality. He believed I would *potentially* be unfaithful to him if anything ever happened to him *(just as in the movie we were watching)*. Appalled that he could insinuate such filth, I challenged him, and as we argued, he called me a prostitute.

That was below the belt, even for James! Some things do sting and have stung over the years, but that was so wrong on every level. I could not believe he had said that. Why would he ever call me, the mother of his precious son, that? Worse of all, it was in front of our son too!

Right from our pre-marital days, I had never done anything to make him doubt my faithfulness and he had never ever caught me two-timing as it is not in my nature to do such a thing. I was dumbfounded. Why, why? What have I done to be labelled as such? I asked myself.

I was too shocked to give him a reply, so, without further ado, I simply left him and Jamie in the living room and went to bed. In retrospect, I could not sleep, but I kept pondering over his harsh label amidst tears.

In my opinion, James's paranoia was due to his insecurities, and his inferiority complex was because of his joblessness and his inability to look after his family properly. I also put it down to guilt as a result of the atrocities he had meted out to me in the past and was still capable of carrying out.

The next morning I lay awake in bed with Jamie sleeping between us. Realising James was awake, I decided to sit upright by resting my back against the headboard. Then I managed to *fling* him a good morning, even though I was still raging inside from the previous night's episode.

James mumbled a reply. Afterwards, when I could no longer bear it, I confronted him by asking, 'Honey, why did you call me a prostitute yesterday? Have I ever had an affair with your father, brother or any male member of your fam...?'

Before I could finish my statement, I felt a heavy thump across the left hand side of my face which practically knocked the breath out of me. Briefly, I saw a bright vision of tiny stars, followed by a deafening and eerie noise. The pain was agonising. I thought it was impossible to feel that kind of agony and survive.

I had no knowledge of exactly what he had struck me with or the extent of the damage done to me, until I went to the hospital to find out. James had slapped me and burst my left eardrum, which caused a blood clot. As a result, to this day, almost 17 years on, I cannot answer a phone using my left ear. I often feel pain and sometimes hear strange eerie sounds. Again, he apologised and I never reported it to the police.

★ ★ ★

I was not a perfect wife, but I was a faithful and good one. I loved James with all my heart, but had never bargained for the abuse I was subjected to. Sometimes, I would count the days and thank God that there had not been any fights or quarrels between us for a couple of days. Funnily enough, just as I would be celebrating and feeling glad in my mind, there would be one brewing. Such was my life with James.

Occasionally, he was nice, kind and jovial, just like the good times, but only always as nice as pie and charming to me when people were round or whenever we visited someone, which was very rare.

James was not the stereotypical abuser, therefore, nobody would ever believe me if I told them what an angry brute he was most of the time at home. It was as though he were two peculiar individuals with different characters; like *Dr Jekyll and Mr. Hyde*. At times, his paranoia would get the better of him which was the main reason we hardly ever went out together. As a result, we constantly ended up quarrelling or fighting on the way and I always ended up worse for it.

What's more, when I did go out with him, I had to button my shirts or tops right up to my neck to avoid exposing any part of my body or skin, even in the hot summer weather. It was so sad that I often wondered what had caused him to have such a change in character. I initially deceived myself that it was because he loved me and I continually made excuses for his weaknesses, faults and his ill-treatment of me.

Back in Nigeria, never had he behaved in such a manner or shown any jealous or abusive traits, otherwise I would have left without giving him a second thought.

★ ★ ★

In 1995, we had a big row and he ended up punching me mercilessly while I was carrying Jamie in my arms. As he lashed out, one of his blows that were intended for me mistakenly landed on Jamie. This surprised me because I never thought he would beat me while I had Jamie with me.

James only stopped when my poor baby screamed, which was when James realised he had hit him. Even then, I could not put Jamie down, fearing that he would continue to punch away at me if I did. I held Jamie close to me *(he was terrified and was still screaming non-stop)*, while I tried to comfort him as we were both crying. James then tried to take him from me in order to console him, but I would not let go of Jamie.

'What else are you going to do, Incredible Hulk?' I said, 'Punch us some more?'

He ignored me, so I stood up and took Jamie with me to another room. I could condone him beating me, but not Jamie. At that moment in time, I feared for him, so I called the police who notified Social Services and James was arrested.

When two female Social Services officials arrived, I narrated the incident to them and they immediately decided to pursue the case further. Again, my courage failed me. I lacked the will power and foolishly could not go ahead with it due to the stupid love I still felt for James.

Deep down, I could not bear to press charges against James. Stupid was my middle name. I was helplessly and hopelessly in love with being in love. My self-confidence was non-existent and love had taken leave of my brain and senses. I could not bear to see James go to prison.

Despite my initial fear, I honestly believed in my heart that he would never intentionally hit or hurt Jamie. He truly felt very bad for the mistaken punch and the reality was, even though James did not love me as I loved him, he loved our son, but under the influence, I would not put anything past him.

Not long after, he went out as usual, and came back late which would not usually have bothered me because I was used to it. The problem was that he was supposed to buy a few food items on his way back for me to cook as I had no money.

After waiting all afternoon without hearing from him, I called my very good friend Sarena and asked her to bring us some food. Originally from Sierra Leone, Sarena is a very pretty and petite mixed heritage stunner, who lived in our neighbourhood. Unfortunately, she had no cooked food in the house, and as she was unable to drive at the time, she gave her younger brother, Sammy, some money to buy us some Kentucky Fried Chicken *(KFC)*.

Sammy, also mixed of heritage, is an extremely good-looking hunk of a man. Just like a younger brother to me, he was always very pleasant, polite and respectful. Sammy was dating my younger sister, Michelle.

Sammy arrived within half an hour and he took us in his car to the KFC *drive thru*. When we got there, he asked us to choose what we wanted and even insisted on buying some for James too. He wanted to save me the trouble of having to cook for James as it was already late in the evening.

I thanked him for the food as he dropped us in front of our house and then, he drove off. I grabbed a fork from the kitchen to eat my chicken *(to prevent food from lodging in my long nails)* and within a couple of minutes, James walked in as Jamie and I were eating. I welcomed him and narrated how Sarena had given Sammy some money to buy KFC for all of us.

'We were hungry honey', I said as I gobbled up my KFC, while pointing to his food. I had removed the food from its paper packaging and presented it nicely for him on a plate, which was now covered on the table.

James looked at the food with disgust and then back at me with stark hatred in his eyes. To say he was angry would be an understatement, as he began to throw verbal abuse at me, non-stop.

I could not take it anymore, so I said, 'James, I know you are looking for a fight this evening, but kindly allow me to eat this food in peace first. When I am done, I will give to you the fight that you want as I can't fight you on an empty stomach.'

'You stupid and shameless woman', James replied. 'Sammy only bought it because he is trying to get into your knickers.' *That was the unkindest cut of all!*

As I opened my mouth in an attempt to respond, he shushed me and threatened to slap the taste of the KFC from off my tongue if I dared to utter a single word. I was so shocked and angry that the fork I was holding in my hand was shaking. I had lost my appetite.

Although appalled by his accusations and advice, what he had said still registered. I obeyed and did not utter another word, as any attempt would have led to further abuse and another round of beatings from the Incredible Hulk. I truly could not go through any more and I knew better by now so I went to bed in tears and resumed my normal routine of crying myself to sleep.

He did not go out the following day, but instead, he stayed at home to continue his abuse from where he had left off the previous day. After another round of *mouth almighty's* tongue lashing sessions, he started making accusatory remarks. Shouting, he said, 'Sammy is your lover and he is always here when I am away', then he continued furiously, 'I will break both your bones and Sammy's the next time he comes anywhere near you or whenever I set eyes upon him.' *All hail Sammy, wow! Two sisters. Ain't you lucky, I thought!*

'You cheap tart', James continued disgustedly, 'I know you would spread your legs just for a piece of chicken. Whore!' *That was the final straw. The low blow. It wounded me mentally.*

I could not bear the immoral insults any longer, so I confronted him by saying, 'James, the gas tank in your brain is running a bit low right now. Deep down, in your heart of hearts, you know that I am a faithful and devoted wife to you. You are only accusing and tormenting me to make yourself feel better, due to your own unfaithfulness and all the atrocities you have committed. So, do not judge me by your own standards, okay!'

James was shocked that I had dared to speak to him in that manner, let alone say those things. He then turned his head to look behind him, possibly to check if someone else was speaking on my behalf. Even so, once I had started there was no holding back. I continued, but made sure there was a wide distance between us in the living room.

'Do you know how demeaning it was to call Sarena to ask her for food? I only called her because I didn't know when or whether *your majesty* would honour us with his presence. James, were you, or were you not fully aware that there was nothing in the house for your son and I to eat when you left home this morning?' *I had concluded that my time of death at his hands was getting closer, so what did I have to lose? Nothing. I had to go all the way!*

James said nothing, but I could see that he was already blowing up and was about to explode. I did not care!

Angrily, I shouted at him, 'You normally return home between 2.00a.m. and 4.00a.m., so how was I to know you were going to be slightly earlier this time? Am I psychic?' I asked him, *although, I was wondering whose pair of balls I had grown within the hour.*

'What really what your intention James? For us to starve to death? Whose responsibility is it to provide food for your wife and kid? Sammy's? You sick, perverted bastard?' *Even if he was going to kill me, I would die happy knowing that I had stood up to him and had offloaded all the pent-up emotions, anger and frustration repressed in my mind.*

The pair of balls I grew earlier belonged to James. A bit of role reversal was what he needed. I had stripped him of his command and his manhood, and I had taken possession of them both in my bare hands. He wanted them back before I crushed them; he had to retrieve them from me, and fast!

Suddenly, like a wounded lion, he advanced towards me, but, before he could get to me, I ran into the bathroom and locked the door behind me. He started pounding and banging on the door, asking me to give him back his wedding since, as he claimed, I had been unfaithful to him.

Anger is the root of most evil. James was angry and his anger was explosive. Whenever he got irate, everyone and everything around us felt it. In the course of James's explosive anger, everything shatters even if he does not touch or hit them. There was always collateral damage externally and *internally in my case!* This occasion was no exception. He sounded deranged and was acting like a mad man.

I was so scared. Jamie was crying in our bedroom and the door was nearly coming off its hinges as he was banging very loudly and shaking it violently.

Aware of the damage he was capable of doing to me if he succeeded in pulling the door down, I tried to take off the ring. Unfortunately, the ring was difficult to take off because it was tight. *I had given birth (mother's muscles) and gained a few pounds since my marriage.*

Unlike James who conveniently claimed that he had lost his wedding ring, mine had never been off my finger since James placed it there. Anyway, since he wanted it now, I would give it to him and I vowed to myself that I would even cut off my finger if I had to, just to give him back his sham of a stupid ring.

James was still pounding on the door and in my panic, I tried to find an alternative escape route, but the bathroom window was very small. Despite wriggling, twisting and turning my finger repeatedly, the ring would not come off.

All of a sudden, it occurred to me to use soap, which helped a great deal and the ring slid off my finger, onto the floor. I picked it up and quietly, but unexpectedly, unlocked the bathroom door. James was dumbfounded when I handed him the ring and then I walked towards the living room.

Pretending I was about to sit down on the sofa, I bolted for the front door, opened it quickly and did an Usain instead. I can say that, at that precise moment in time, not even Bolt would have been able to catch me had he tried!

The door slammed shut behind me, my keys were inside the house, but I did not care. The demon in him had reappeared, just like the first time he had beaten me. I did not dare to use the house phone to call the police, as he would have killed me before they arrived. I also did not risk taking Jamie with me; for to do so would have provoked him even more. On the other hand, I knew for sure that he would not hurt his son.

I ran to the nearest public payphone, dialled 999 and a female voice answered. She spoke softly as I asked for the police and then, everything got to me; I lost it and I broke down, sobbing uncontrollably.

James had not hit me, but I felt as if he had killed me. What I was going through at that particular moment was a fate worse than death. I was an emotional mess and a wreck. Still holding onto the phone receiver, the woman at the other end of the line asked me to be calm and to stay on the line as the police would be with me before I finished my conversation with her. She was correct!

Within a few minutes, a police car with two officers arrived at the phone booth. As soon as I briefed the officers about my plight, they took me home in their car and knocked on our front door.

James answered the door and the police officers informed him that I had invited them because we'd had some misunderstandings. He ushered them in, asked them to take a seat and cheekily asked me to offer them tea or coffee since I had invited them. The officers told James that they were not there to drink, but rather, to sort things out, and then asked James if he had something to say.

'Yes', James answered, 'just a few words.'

'Go ahead, what is it then sir?' The other police officer asked, getting ready to jot something down in his notepad.

'No and comment.' James replied, and then he muttered under his breath that he had no time for them, as he attempted to make his way to the bedroom upstairs. The police officers heard him, noticed what an arrogant and angry clown he was, and called for backup. I went into our bedroom to check on Jamie, who was no longer crying, but asleep. I gave him a kiss and tiptoed out of the room so as not to disturb him, then went back downstairs into the living room.

Within a few minutes, more police officers arrived in a police van and after a bit of a scuffle, the officers overpowered, handcuffed and bundled James into the van, just as he was; without shoes, for he had none on. He resisted arrest and had foolishly attempted to fight the officers. *Thank God, he had slept through the hullabaloo.*

While James was being taken away, two officers, a male and female, stayed behind to ensure I was okay. They asked me if I wanted to press charges against James but I told them I was only interested in having him out of my life forever.

The police officers advised me to go somewhere else as they envisaged that we would not be safe when James was released the next morning. I had refused to press charges, and just in case James, the violent man, decided to take his *pound of flesh,* they offered to put us in sheltered accommodation. After thanking them, I mentioned that I would rather go and stay with my Mum and siblings in Manchester. Mum, Maxwell, Gezza and Michael had since relocated to Manchester in 1994, Christine moved to Florida with her husband and twin daughters, while Gloria, Michelle and I lived in London. Dad also left London in 1994 to join Steppy and my half-brothers in Nigeria.

The female officer advised me to notify the local police station in Manchester about the matter in hand on our arrival. This was necessary in order to remove James immediately if he came within a short distance of us. She also asked if I had anyone who could stay with us for the night, so I gave her Sarena's number, who she called.

Sarena was with us in no time and she helped me pack my bags. Jamie had since woke up, and much later, after I had fed, washed and put him to bed, I told Sarena all that had transpired, amid floods of tears as she tried to console me.

A few minutes later, she called Sammy and asked him to be at my house at 5.30a.m. the next morning, to drive us to Euston train station for our onward journey to Manchester. That night I did not sleep a wink as I had so much on my mind.

★ ★ ★

It was 5.20a.m. the next day. We heard keys turning in the keyhole of the front door and someone was shaking the door violently. On hearing the keys, Sarena and I panicked.

'James has come home. The police had let him out early.' I began to cry, knowing that James would kill me without batting an eyelid for planning to leave him and for wanting to take Jamie with me.

I immediately picked Jamie up and said 'Toilet, quick.' We made a dash for it and decided to lock ourselves in there. In my panic, I forgot that I had bolted all the doors from the inside and locked all the windows when Sarena arrived, and just before the police officers left.

Fear and terror gripped me and I almost wet myself! I was not thinking straight until Sarena reminded me of something, saying, 'How could James have gotten in, when everywhere was locked?' Silly me, for that never even crossed my mind. Such is the power of fear!

It was Sammy! He arrived at my front door and decided to play a stupid prank on us. He had inserted his car keys into the keyhole and shook the front door briskly as if he was my landlord. Hoping that he had succeeded in scaring us, Sammy decided to knock on the door and then spoke through the raised letterbox. I was still convinced it was James and I would not leave the toilet, but Sarena asked me to stay calm while she checked. She was not as scared of James, although she looked through the window first, to make sure it really was Sammy.

Seeing it was, she opened the door to let him in, locked it behind them and called out to me to confirm it was Sammy. I came out of the toilet to find Sarena hailing insults and throwing everything she could lay her hands on at him. I do not condone violence but I took off the black-feathered flip-flops I was wearing which was only feather-weight and threw them at Sammy. He was wise enough to plead for mercy, but only from afar.

What a stupid boy! If only he knew what an awful prank that was and at my expense too. He apologised and promised not to do anything like that again. Still, Sammy being the clown that he was, made light of the matter by joking about it and laughed at the effect it had had on us, as he drove us all to Euston station.

Sarena paid our train fare to Manchester. Broke and broken-hearted, I had no self-esteem or dignity left. James had stripped me of everything and I became his fool and slave-woman! The only bit of sanity I had left was in knowing and making sure that my child and I were safe and as far away from James as possible.

The fact that James had been locked up did not stop me from being terrified. I was so scared and messed up, both psychologically and emotionally that I would not get on the train unless Sarena and Sammy checked inside the train thoroughly. In my mind's eye, James seemed to possess the power of ubiquity or omnipresence. He could appear and reappear in front of us at will *(and if he did, that would be the end of me)*.

Jamie and I got on the train, but only after Sarena and Sammy assured me repeatedly that James was not there. They had checked the train from top to bottom and coach to coach, to make sure James was not on it. I thanked them both for being so wonderful, then hugged and waved them good-bye.

My Mum and siblings were already at the train station waiting to pick us up and I broke down and cried when I saw them. Mum wept when I told her briefly what I had been through with James and she was shocked that I had not confided in her until then. All the same, she understood and forgave me when I told her my reasons.

On our way, we called in at the local police station to notify them about my situation as advised. Thereafter, we headed straight for home, but guess who was waiting outside Mum's house?

Chapter Seventeen:
A Mirage

It was the devil, James! On spotting him, I instantly felt horror. Shocked and terrified, I immediately recalled my fears at the train station. For this same reason, I had insisted that Serena and Sammy search the whole train thoroughly, knowing what James was capable of doing. I became convinced then that James was channelling with the devil and that he possessed the power of *everywhereness*. Either that or he had travelled on the same train as us, but had chosen not to be seen by us.

James made a big fuss about us going back with him. *Why? Did he miss us? Had he only just realised what he'd lost?* Without thinking twice, I called the police who arrived immediately and asked him to leave.

He left, only to return three days later, after midnight and when I least expected him. Wondering who it was at that time of night, I opened the door to see James on his hands and knees *(like the dog that he was),* crying out loud like a baby, begging and disturbing the whole neighbourhood. It was raining, he refused to leave and it was quite embarrassing.

I threatened to call the police again, but he was adamant that he would not get up or leave until I had heard him out. James was certain that the police would only ask him to leave or escort him away, but he added cheekily that nothing would stop him from returning later.

In some kind of twisted way he was correct, so it was pointless for me to insist that I would call the police. Moreover, he was determined that I should hear what he had to say. Mum was urging, nudging and persuading me to invite him in to talk things over since I already had a son by him. It was still raining heavily and I felt sorry for him. Overcome with sympathy, I let him in!

We talked until the early hours of the morning. I reminded him about all that I had been through with him, pinpointing the fact that my most *critical error* was giving him a second chance the first time he had beaten me. Had I taken action then, he would never have done it again, which, I stressed to him, was the reason I was doing what I was doing now.

I later asked him why and how he would change now. Was there any excuse for his abuse? If there was, what was it? He could not explain. He was up the *creek* and he knew it. Instead, he remained silent, but felt very bad and promised *again* that he would change.

He then vowed, firstly, never, ever to lay his hands on me *again,* a promise he had made numerous times before, but had always broken. This time, he insisted it was going to be different because he actually swore on his parents' lives. Secondly, he promised to ditch all of his friends in London *(according to him, they were responsible for his wayward behaviour*) and thirdly, we would start afresh in Manchester. He assured me that the only time he would go to London would be to pack our belongings and he would return with them to Manchester on the same day.

Although he swore on his parents' lives, that was not convincing enough. Further still, I did not believe he would not beat me anymore, but one thing I knew for sure, was that he had no friends in Manchester to go out with, so I agreed with him. I clearly forgot that a leopard cannot change its spots and that he could pick new friends who might have an even worse influence on him.

I did not talk about his *dope* and drinking problem, as well as the late nights, which were the worst part of the matter. I deceived myself that we could work on those issues by seeing a specialist. This was because I saw a glimmer of hope for the realisation of my age-long dream; of Jamie being raised by both of his parents in an ideal home, environment and situation.

I detested the thought of ever being classed as a *single mother* or *single parent*. I ignorantly thought that I would rather die than be referred to as one, since in our African community, such women are often labelled as *loose*.

It was going to be a slippery slope, but one I was willing to climb for the sake of love. Also, I was prepared to get bitten by the same dog severally, for Jamie's sake.

The mind-boggling questions I would have loved to ask myself at the time, which I now also know the whole world is curious to know the answers to are: 'Why did I not leave him the first time he hit me? Why did I keep receiving the beatings? Why did I keep forgiving him and lastly, why did I not punish him by sending him to jail where he belonged so he could rot?'

Look out for my simple and sincere answer towards the end of this book.

* * *

James stayed with us at Mum's house, he helped take care of Jamie and we were quite a happy family unit again. Mum was glad to see me smile once more and the happy days began to return. Luckily, we were allocated a new build home within a few months.

James then hired a van, went to London for our belongings and returned with them the same day as he had promised. I was glad. Everything was sorted and we settled in our new home. James truly did curb his ways and lifestyle, he helped at home and he was also *actively* seeking employment.

Jamie was getting older and I intended to fulfil my life-long ambition of becoming an entrepreneur, so I was busy doing some research. Mum told me about a Business Start-up Course running locally and I immediately enrolled for it. On completion of the course, I created a business plan, gathered a few savings together, combined with some funding from the Prince's Trust and I eventually opened my Beauty & Lingerie Shop called Reneez.

We found a Beacon Catholic School for Jamie and while he was at school, I put everything I had into making my shop a success by retailing and wholesaling beauty products. I also held beauty and fashion shows in exclusive venues to boost profits.

A friend of a friend of mine spoke to some people who ran a pirate radio station and they agreed to do a jingle to advertise the name and shop, Reneez. The jingle was advertised regularly on their radio station and I was very proud. At some point, frequent listeners started to tune in to answer quizzes in order to win tickets for my forthcoming shows. Our free local newspaper called The Advertiser also helped to advertise Reneez.

James was initially supportive, but later became more insecure, paranoid, obsessive and abusive. The dark and ugly side of him started to come out of its hiding place *again*. It was only early days at the shop, I was still struggling, and I was no Martha Stewart *(a lifestyle guru and businesswoman)*, but neither was I rich.

He could not handle the fact that I was doing something useful and worthwhile by taking control and finally making something of my life. James made a habit of discouraging me from attending various meetings or seminars to develop and better myself. *'You do not need them. They are a complete waste of time', Negative Nathan would often say.* He thrived on giving me backhanded compliments wrapped up in sarcasm. Rather than helping to build me up and encourage me, James derived absolute pleasure in gradually breaking me down.

A while later, I did stand up to him by letting him know that, *not* only was I *not* going to allow him to hinder my progress, I also *refused* to be controlled and manipulated. I reminded him that I am a fully-grown adult, capable of making my *own* mind up and my own decisions, no matter how much I valued his opinion.

Despite James's disapproval, I took it upon myself to attend only the most important seminars without his consent. As a result, he never hit me for it, but he would either blank me or play mind games for days. *It hurt so bad and I rather wished he had hit me!*

★ ★ ★

It was a beautiful summer's day in 1996. While we were preparing for one of my forthcoming fashion shows, a big concert featuring the Fugees *(an American hip-hop group)* was due to take place the following day at the O2 Apollo Manchester *(formerly the Manchester Apollo)*. It was two days to my show and I decided to hire some local boys to distribute more leaflets around Manchester and at the Apollo. I had previously printed and distributed a lot of posters and leaflets in Manchester but I wanted to take extra advantage of the concert by reaching out to thousands more *(besides the adverts/jingles on radio)*.

At 10.00a.m. the next day, which was also the day of the Fugees event, James and the boys left to distribute the leaflets. When they ran out, the boys came back to the shop to ask me for some more leaflets as James was nowhere to be found. He had driven off with the bulk of the leaflets in the car boot after dropping the boys off in Piccadilly, promising to return within the hour.

That was news to me so I tried to reach him on his mobile phone, but it was switched off. The plan was for them to hand out leaflets to a lot of people in the

Manchester city centre area, before going to Ardwick Green to target the queues outside the Apollo from 4.00p.m. I was devastated and disappointed.

It was after 2.00p.m. but I thought that if I could get through to James now, the boys would still make it to the Apollo for 4.00p.m. or just after. James had the leaflets sitting in the car and he could not be reached! There had to be a good explanation. On the other hand, James was no fool. He knew exactly what he was doing.

The clock was ticking. No James, no leaflets! To utilise their time, the boys later distributed the few leaflets that I had left in the shop locally and I gave them their full pay, even though they had only done half of the job. This was on the condition that they would be on standby in case I needed them again that day. The boys were willing to work and they were not to blame.

I checked the time. It was 3.18p.m. I knew James would be on his way to pick Jamie up from school at 3.30p.m. and would then drop him off to me at the shop. At 4.00p.m. James did not bring Jamie, nor did he answer his mobile or the house phone. I started to panic and decided to go home. After putting away the signs outside the shop, I cashed the till, locked the shop door and made my way home on foot. We had one car between us, but our house was only between 10 to 15 minutes walk from the shop.

The car was parked on our drive. James and Jamie were at home, thank God! Jamie was eating his dinner, but as soon as he saw me, he ran up to me with a big smile on his face. I picked him up, smiling and giving him kisses at the same time.

I greeted James too, who only nodded his head without saying a word and then I sat down to feed Jamie. After thanking James for picking Jamie up, I mentioned that I had been trying to get in touch with him to check he was okay, and to get some more leaflets since the boys had run out hours ago.

'What on earth happened James? I was worried. Where have you been?'

James's reply was, 'Well, I went to pick up our son from school.' *Of course, it only took a whole day to do that, I thought to myself.*

'The leaflets are in the boot, go and get them, and listen; it's your turn to look after Jamie now, so you take over because I'm going out.' James said aggressively as though we were fighting or I had annoyed him previously. If I had, I was not aware of it.

I looked at him and said, 'James, you said the leaflets are in the boot, which means they have been sitting there all day. You know how big this event is and I don't want to miss the multitude of people queuing out there.' Looking at the time, 'A quarter to five', I said, 'I will get the leaflets and call the boys back to pick them up, as they may still be able to find some big queues.' With that I stood up, as I had finished feeding Jamie.

I grabbed the car keys from the table and walked towards the front door but James got up, pulled me back and said, 'Where are you going? Did I not tell you to stay and look after Jamie? I said it's your turn; now, not next year!'

'But I...' I was stopped in my tracks as James grabbed me by my hair and dragged me back into the living room and onto the couch. I was shocked and screamed angrily as I attempted to get up, but he pushed me back on the couch and then, hit me. I got up again and we started to fight. I fell back on the couch yet again as we fought, and my punches, if I got any in, must have been lightweight compared to his heavyweight ones. I could smell the dreadful stench of wakibaki on his person but he was not drunk. *Well, I could be wrong!*

As usual, I could not help the fact that Jamie had witnessed it. He was already crying, but that did not stop James, as he continued punching me on the couch. My revenge was to grab hold of the lovely silk shirt he had recently purchased and to keep hold of it. I was glad. When he saw the large rip in his shirt and noticed a couple of buttons missing too, he dealt me a knockout blow and he was done.

That did not faze me. I was used to it and although I was dying inside, I did not want to give him the satisfaction of seeing me cry any longer. He went upstairs to change, came back downstairs within minutes and picked up the car keys, which had fallen on the floor when he dragged me.

Afterwards, he walked out without uttering a single word, shut the door behind him and drove off with the leaflets still in the boot. *Perhaps he was going to hand out the leaflets at the Apollo.*

When James had gone upstairs, I reached out to Jamie who was still crying. He came to me and I hugged him and tried to console him even though I had tears in my eyes too. As James left, I looked in the mirror, saw the terrible state of my face, and decided to cancel my show. My event was the following day and I would need to cancel the food preparations at Mum's end too, so I called her to explain what had happened.

'My face is all mashed up, I have no car, a million things left to do and no help. How am I going to carry on with the arrangements? I have to cancel my show, Mum.'

Mum said, 'No way my daughter, you have spent a lot of money and have worked way too hard for this. This is the devil's doing but the show must go on.' Always the voice of reason, my Mum. 'You are not alone, you have your family, and we are here to help you. Always remember that.'

'Never mind all the money I have spent. My mind is not in the right place now and I can't concentrate.'

'You'll have to come over. Leave it with me', Mum said. 'I'll ask Max to pick you up within the hour.'

'That's very nice of you Mum, but no thank you. It's not that bad and I'll be fine.' I was in a bad way but I did not want anyone to see me in that state.

'If it's bad enough for you to cancel your show, then it is bad! Are you sure you are truly alright? Anyway, whatever you say. Just call me if you need anything. Goodnight dear.'

'Don't worry, I'll take a couple of paracetamol tablets and go to sleep. Goodnight Mum and thank you again for everything.' My head was banging from James pulling my hair, but I did not tell her that.

Mum spoke to Max, Mike, Gezza and my Cousin Billy, who all called to make sure I was okay and they promised to help me with the running around and arrangements. James never came home.

The following day my family arrived as promised, but went back home to get ready for the show after they had helped me. Afterwards, I got myself and Jamie dressed, hid my bruised *(by now panda eyes)* face underneath heavy make-up, put on my dark sunglasses and as soon as my family returned to pick us, we all left for the venue.

Despite the distress, the show went on. James walked in as a guest, cheekily moved the ticket collector from his position, and positioned himself there instead, collecting the tickets and cash. *Hey Mr Downer, don't rain on my parade! For someone who loves money that much, I wondered why he had never got a job.* Seeing him sat there, I advised him to *not* only have a great time *rolling* in it all, but also to *knock himself out* while he was at it. He ignored me.

The turnout was great even without the Fugees crowd that I had received the beatings for. My brothers wanted to have James beaten up but I warned them that unless they were going to kill him completely, they should not dare lay a finger on him because if unsuccessful, my fate would be worse than death. My brothers left it. They were not ready to become murderers. *Yet!*

My show was a success and I was very happy. The customers loved my designs. They continued to purchase items after the show had ended and even while we were packing up. It was my most successful show ever. Thank God I did not cancel it. James apologised, but he never told me where he spent the night or where he had dumped the leaflets. Even so, I had no choice but to forgive him. I was too happy to bear any grudges and I thanked my wonderful family, especially my rock of a Mum who was the motivating force behind it all. She also had Jamie throughout the event.

★ ★ ★

After the show, James became irrational and then he got more delusional and paranoid by the day. Each time salesmen came over to pitch their latest product lines for me to sell in my shop, James was always very suspicious. He was forever accusing me of befriending them, stating they were my boyfriends pretending to be sales representatives. I do not know where he got his ideas from because I bet there were no more than two or three at the most in a whole year. Besides, I always ensured they were from reputable companies who came by appointment only.

Perhaps he was referring to the few, who often popped their heads in through the shop door to market a few stolen goods or pirated DVDs; the kind you find everywhere, but who I always turned away. I never bothered arguing with James since I knew he was wrong.

On one fateful day, he embarrassed and made a scapegoat of one sales representative; a poor, old bald-headed man, probably in his sixties or even older. Armed with his catalogue, the salesman was busy pitching his products to me as James walked in. Without any pleasantries or questioning, James grabbed the catalogue from the man's lap, threw it on the floor and ordered him out of the shop. The man stood up, but looked on in shock and horror.

What kind of man is this? A mad one? Judging from the puzzled look on his poor, wrinkly face, he must have been dying to ask those questions out loud but knew better, as James was behaving like a recently discharged psychiatric patient. I bet the old chap could not believe what was going on.

It was a huge display of disgusting! I was highly ashamed, but quickly apologised to the man, who wanted to notify the police. I informed him that he was my husband and then helped him to pick his documents up from the floor. *Did I feel like Abigail when she was trying to pacify David, who was riding down to Nabal's house to punish him for being an ingrate!*

The man left immediately after promising to put in a complaint. I guess he thought that James was a husband that was blinded and enraged by jealousy and therefore, he did not want to become involved or entangled in a family dispute.

James was a coward as he knew how to pick his victims by taking advantage of the fact that the man was old and feeble. He must have guessed that the elderly man would not have been able to throw a punch at him if the argument between them degenerated into fisticuffs. *Where was he when all the young, buff, sales clerks or DVD chaps came knocking at the door or popping in?*

James, defending his actions to me, asked, 'If he was a salesman, where were his products? I saw no creams, shampoos or other things!'

'They were in paper form; something called erm... *a catalogue.*' I said sarcastically, still dismayed by his inexcusable behaviour.

'If you had bothered to ask or check before flinging his things on the floor, you would have seen them.' I replied, shaking my head in disgust. 'It was only a sales pitch, not a delivery of products, for heaven's sake.'

James was embarrassed and there was nothing else he could say. Instead, he shot a quick glance at his watch, opened the door and left without apologising *(although, not before helping himself to some cash from the till).* He must have realised it was almost time for him to pick Jamie up from school.

The next day, I telephoned to offer my apologies to the gentleman and his company, and the matter was resolved.

On another occasion, while I was attending to a female customer in the shop, James burst in. I said a quick 'Hi' to him, and he said 'Hi' back to me, then headed straight for the till, which he opened and shut immediately. He called me aside to ask for some money, and because I asked him to wait until I had finished dealing with my customer, he started to insult me.

He then got very angry, ordered the customer out of the shop and locked the door. Afterwards, he headed towards me and as we were arguing *(because I was unhappy that he had the cheek to order my customer out)*, he slapped me hard across the face.

A number of passers-by from outside *(including the would-be customer)* could see us quarrelling through the glass doors and within a matter of minutes, a small crowd had gathered to watch. The slap was no big deal as I was used to it, but it stopped me from arguing, and I stepped back, cupping my slapped right cheek in my right palm without uttering another word.

He continued to ramble as he was verbally *incontinent,* but I was not bothered and did not listen, for I was past caring. When one of the spectators who were watching the *free show* saw him slap me informed the police, I lied that it was a lover's tiff that had been sorted, and the officer left.

I knew why he *needed* money. *For his fix!* He was surprised and infuriated that there was insufficient money in the till, not taking into account that it was quite early *(just a little after 10.30a.m.)* and we had not had many sales.

James had humiliated me in the shop *yet again* in front of a potential customer and an audience. It was my name above the shop and James did not give *two hoots* about that or me. Had James been in his right mind and waited patiently, perhaps that customer might have bought the items she wanted and he would have got the money he needed to buy his stuff.

★ ★ ★

In all sincerity, he did not have as many friends in Manchester but he always had someplace to go and still kept late nights out. I was almost certain that James's aim in life was to put me down continuously, as it seemed like he thrived on my unhappiness. We fought almost every other day, both at home and in the shop so much so that I felt I might have to keep a pair of boxing gloves by my bedside even as I slept.

Curtains are not soundproof, neither are all walls. No doubt, our neighbours often saw or heard pounding on the walls amid screaming and shouting matches. They were certainly aware of the *epidemic* forever brewing behind our closed doors, but they could do nothing about it besides calling the police. However, each time the police came, I still could not press any charges due to shame, scandal, stupidity and *love*. The fact that I had my business did not help matters.

Things went from bad to worse, progressively worse, that I could no longer bear it. Living with daily downs; the verbal and physical abuse damaged my self-esteem. James was forever calling me a fool to the extent that I had to ask my Mum one day, saying, 'Mum please, as my mother, I want you to answer this question honestly because I would like to know. Am I really a fool?'

'No my daughter, you are not.' Close to tears, she said, 'Out of all my children, you are one of the cleverest. Queen Idia, remember?' That's Mum, my best friend and great confidence booster, always making me feel better about myself. Yet, it never lasted long, as James was always around the corner ready to crush those good feelings; making me feel ten times worse.

It was as if I made a deal with the devil and I was living with the enemy. I could do nothing else but live only for my son. Usually exhausted from constantly sobbing in frustration, I resigned myself to his abuse, which I thought I had already become accustomed to. What's more, I started to believe that I was truly *stupid, useless* and actually deserved his abuse, because if I didn't, why was I still harbouring him and his filth? *I can now only presume I was waiting for him to finish me off!*

Chapter Eighteen:
Escape to Freedom

Mum's younger sister, Auntie Florence, came to visit us from New York and we were ecstatic, as we had not seen her in almost ten years. She stayed at Mum's house for the duration of her stay but I was very glad when she visited me in my shop one day. I asked after her children and as we got chatting, recalling the good old days in Nigeria, I remembered that she and her husband were once young lovers. Then out of the blue, I asked her if it was healthy to constantly argue and fight when married.

She was both surprised and shocked that I had asked such an unexpected question, but at the same time, she was curious to know if all was well with my family. For some strange reason, I thought that because she was closer to me in age than my Mum and since she was very much in love with her husband, just as I was with James, she would be able to understand my plight if I opened up to her.

Sensing our conversation was going to carry on for a little while longer, I got up to reverse the *open* sign hanging outside on the glass door and also to lock the door to prevent James from sneaking up on us or eavesdropping.

'All is well but...' I tried to assure her, although, judging by my body language and tone, she must have guessed that all was not well as I walked back to my seat after locking the door. I tried to avoid eye contact with her.

'What is the matter?' Auntie Flo asked insistently, confusion written all over her lovely face. *Poor woman, I thought. I bet she had not anticipated this when she decided to visit her big sister who she had not seen for so long!*

Auntie Flo had *sussed* me out; she knew something was amiss and there was no holding back now. She was certainly not going to let it drop and I needed to ask her the questions filling my mind, so I had no choice but to *spill*.

As I opened my mouth, the questions came rolling out. 'I feel like I am confused about everything at the moment Auntie. I know that marriage is for better or worse, but is it normal for it to be worse almost all the time Auntie Flo? Is it okay to constantly receive beatings from a loved one or anyone else, for that matter?'

At this point, my voice was quivering and hot tears were beginning to well up in my eyes as I tried in vain to hold them back. Auntie Flo looked at me and shook her beautiful head in disagreement. She was full of nothing but sympathy and love for me. Nevertheless, she did not need to say anything, as her countenance said it all.

Auntie Flo was very compassionate as she got up from her seat to hug me saying, 'No my dear, it is not meant to be like that. Never mind *constantly*; he must never hit you, *period!* Love does not hurt and if it does, then it is okay to let go.' She added, 'Love is reciprocal. If I love someone who does not love me back, I will pray for God to withdraw that love instantly.' Wise words from a wise woman! *Mum and her sister are very intelligent women, so where did I get my foolishness from?*

Instantly, I felt sorry for myself and cried. Auntie Flo did not try to stop me but encouraged me to let it all out. By crying, I was crushing every pent-up feeling; all the years and tears of frustration, foolishness and anger I had kept within me until then. Auntie Flo was right, I felt lighter and more relaxed when I was done and I later told her everything.

Stunned by what she had heard after I had finished, she paused for a while and asked me if I had ever considered living in the United States. I answered by telling her there was no point, since James would still find me, no matter where I went. The only way I could be free of him, I had concluded long ago, was when I was in the grave. In fact, he had affirmed that much.

Prior to leaving London for Manchester, I had threatened to leave him several times, but he called my bluff, calling me a spineless, stupid fool, among other names. What's more, Mr. Mugu often foolishly stated that no man would have me, but on the other hand, he would contradict himself by threatening that if I ever left him, he would not only track me down, but he would also break my bones and then kill me. James further boasted *(slapping his hands on his chest)* about getting away with the crime.

Auntie Flo suggested I should move to America after hearing everything and she advised that on arrival, it would be necessary to inform the authorities at the US port of entry that I was fleeing from an abusive husband. She also assured me that James's details would be noted in the US immigration database as an abuser and he would not be allowed entry into the United States. As a result, it would be impossible for him to reach or to *ever* find Jamie or me. That piece of information was incredible and totally unbelievable to hear, yet, it was such sweet music to my ears. The possibility that there was an alternative to the matrimonial hell I was currently living, was mind-blowing. My heart-to-heart with Auntie Flo made me realise that I could not afford to wait to find out whether James meant to carry out his death threat or not.

Auntie Florence was a Godsend! She said it was imperative I did my homework properly by getting the right information through research, as that was crucial before relocating there. She was almost certain that a travel visa would not be required for Jamie and I, since we were British subjects. More importantly, she promised that not only would Jamie and I live with her, she also vowed that she and her family would protect and support us, with God's help.

That was all I needed. Help on how to leave James and be free with my Jamie! With my mind made up, I decided to plan how to raise the cash for our plane tickets and then I started looking forward to leaving James.

Shortly after this, Auntie Florence went back to the United States, but not before she made me promise that I would stay strong enough to carry out my plan. The only other person who knew about it was Mum. Going to my shop every day, planning secretly and making enquiries at the American Embassy were what I gave my utmost attention to, apart from Jamie. In the process, trying to stash most of the cash from sales and not declaring to James any items that I had sold made me feel like the criminal I was not. The truth was, apart from helping me set up initially, James had not contributed or invested a single penny in the shop, hence the reason my name Reneez was emblazoned outside the shop and not James's.

Frankly, there was no need for me to be accountable or answerable to him about anything concerning the business. I never should have involved him business-wise in the first place, but I did so out of love. Now, I had to plan my escape to freedom before he sent me to an early grave. *Eventually is a long word but thank God, the fool had eventually wised up.*

Having saved enough cash to purchase the plane tickets, including a small amount of money to tide us over in the US, I booked our flights and looked forward to collecting our tickets. Afterwards, I ensured I took great care to prevent James from becoming suspicious. Everything was planned carefully and to be carried out discreetly within one month.

Chapter Nineteen:
New Beginnings/Road To Recovery

Waking up just after 7.00a.m. on the morning of February 5, 1997, I looked out of the window and it was a cold and frosty morning. I took a shower, quickly threw on a pastel pink jumper and a pair of black jeans, and then went into Jamie's room. He was fast asleep and I gently woke him up to give him a bath.

Rather than getting him ready for school, I dressed him in his casual playing clothes and positioned him on our bed to lie down next to James, who was still sleeping. Then, I put on my dressing gown, climbed into bed and pulled up the quilt, covering us all to avoid James noticing we were dressed.

James woke up yawning some ten minutes later *(oblivious to what I was up to)*. Seeing he was awake, I told him that I was not feeling very well and had decided to rest at home with Jamie. I promised to inform his school later and asked James if he would kindly open the shop for me, mentioning he only had to stay for half of the day if he wanted.

He agreed *(he did not need telling twice; James, all by himself in the shop, freedom and money from sales, hmm)* and he happily said it was fine by him. He then asked me if I had taken any pain relieving tablets, to which I replied *no*, but I promised to take some later.

Shortly after, James got out of bed, yawned again, did a couple of stretches by way of exercise, and then went to take a shower. I was still in bed when he had finished and was dressed. When I offered to make him some breakfast, he insisted I stayed in bed since I was unwell and said he would grab something quick from the kitchen downstairs.

James gave us both a peck on our cheeks even though Jamie was fast asleep and I gave him a hug too, and said, 'God bless you.' That was typical of me, since I said it to him every day, to which he answered a quick, 'amen' and then went downstairs to the kitchen.

That was James, forever taking me for granted by answering casually and not taking my prayers or best wishes seriously. Little did he know that it was to be my last blessing to him as his wife.

Minutes later, just before 8.45 a.m., he left to open our shop. As soon as I heard the front door shut and the car engine starting, I immediately jumped out of bed *(I was almost suffocating due to my combination of jumper, dressing gown and quilt)* and looked out of the window to make sure he had gone.

Absolutely certain, I dressed properly, combed my hair and applied my make-up in no time. I woke Jamie up, but he was still sleepy, so I washed his face and changed his clothes. As I put on his shoes, I explained that he was not going to school, but out with me instead. He was happy and had a big smile on his face as I lovingly gave him a peck on each of his smooth, soft round cheeks.

Our flight was at 10.45a.m. and I had booked a taxi the previous day for 9.10a.m. Bearing in mind the limited time I had to get to my Mum's and the airport, I hastily unplugged the house phone to avoid me panicking if it rang *(I knew James would ring)*. Next, I quickly retrieved the letter I had written two days before from its hiding place and scribbled down the name James to address the *Dear James letter*, which I had deliberately kept until when I was ready to leave. It stated:

5 February 1997

Dear James,

I write this letter with a heavy heart to inform you that the hell you have put me through over the years, is neither the kind of life I anticipated nor ever imagined.

In giving you my all, you did nothing but shatter both my love and me into pieces, hence I am picking up what little piece there is left of me and leaving you for good, before you finish me off as you not only threatened, but promised.

I am mighty glad reality finally dawned on me and I am now through with your b.s. However, my considerate nature is the only reason I apologise for taking Jamie with me. He is all I have in the world and I have prayed for God to forgive me.

On the other hand, I also know that God's punishment would be greater if I fail to train up Jamie in the way he should go. You are his biological father, but no role model for him and I do not want my angel to grow up or end up being like you.

For all the late nights you came home, the sleepless nights you put me through, the different types of abuse I tolerated from you, least of all the beatings, my burst eardrum and premature delivery; those I could bear, as they were secondary. What I detest the most and cannot endure is your philandering nature, which my dear is why I am leaving you.

You were smart and I never caught you out, I know, but I knew! Rest assured that there is nothing more powerful than a woman's intuition and I reject any unwanted presents such as Aids, HIV or warts from you. For this reason, I feel justified to state that I love you honey, but not enough to die for you!

As much as it breaks my heart, this note is to inform you that we are going to a place as far away from you as possible, where you will never be able to find us. When Jamie turns 18 it will be up to him to decide whether or not he wants to find you. May God comfort and bless you.

Goodbye.
Irene.

I placed the letter at the foot of the stairs, locked the door and posted all my keys through the letterbox. Holding a little bag firmly in my hand, I carried Jamie over my shoulders and ran as fast as I could to my Mum's house where I had hidden my passport and suitcase *(I'd had Jamie's details previously endorsed on my passport and Mum had recently moved into a house on the next street, which was where I had arranged for the taxi to pick us up from).*

The taxi arrived on time but when I saw the vehicle, I was disappointed. Why in God's name had I been sent a minibus with tinted windows? *Jeez! The devil is a liar.* I needed a car as fast as a *Porsche* to get us to the airport rapidly since we had limited time and I did not want the bubble to burst.

Unbelievably, as we made our way to the airport, I sighted James walking towards our house. I panicked immediately, but quickly ducked down with Jamie and he did not see us. How close was that and while I was attempting to escape? What were the chances of that ever happening? The ubiquitous James again!

At first, I was unhappy it was a taxi minibus, but on the contrary, it provided good camouflage and security due to its glass windows being tinted. Thank God for small mercies and for *tinted glass windows.* God you are incredibly awesome!

I am almost certain that James phoned the house from our shop for some unknown reason. Since there was no response *(as I had unplugged the phone),* his paranoid mind must have led him to believe that I had a boyfriend there with me *(he was always accusing me of two-timing him and he could not have been more wrong).* This might have been why he decided to walk down when I spotted him walking down to what was *our,* well, now his house.

Hypothetically, knowing how James's mind works *(I may be wrong and may God forgive me if I am),* his plan must have been to catch me in the act of my unfaithfulness. James had probably hid the car nearby with the intention of sneaking up on us.

★ ★ ★

Mum accompanied us to the airport and I broke down, sobbing my heart out to her as leaving James was very painful for me. I thought I had mentally checked out from James, but that was apparently not the case. There was no need for me to deceive myself and although I initially tried to hold back the tears in order to be strong, the truth of the matter was that I was still in love with him. Part of me belonged with him. He broke my heart but I still loved him with all the pieces. You do not just fall out of love with someone overnight *(unless the love was never there in the first place).*

The realisation hit me that not only was I walking out of my marriage, I was also ending it and taking his son with me. What could be more cruel? Worse than a she-devil, I was! How could I live with myself after this? I was taking everything away from James. How would he feel? A stab to the heart could not have been more painful.

The *taxi minibus* driver was a bit worried and was about to pull over, wondering what the matter was, but Mum assured him that I was fine and only sad because I was leaving my family behind.

At that stage, I was thinking more about James and what my desertion would do to him. I continued to think more of what I was doing and the effect this would have on him, than about the reason I had decided to flee and was actually fleeing. I wailed deeply out of the love I had for him, for how long I had waited and suffered for him to join me in the UK, and lamented for the love we'd had and shared. Had Mum not been with me, I would have gone back regardless of everything.

Breaking out into an even louder and longer cry, I turned to her and said, 'Mum, I cannot do this, it is unbearable.' It is the most difficult decision I have ever had to make in my life. Mum understood and she tried to console me.

Jamie was crying because his mummy was crying and that broke my heart even more. I had to consider Jamie. I had to be strong for him. He was only three years old, I thought, wiping both his tears and mine. To console him, I then said, 'Jamie darling, we are going away without Daddy for a while, okay, and you may see him later.'

He nodded, but seeing more tears in my eyes, he tried to wipe them away for me and said in his sweet little voice, 'Mummy, why are you crying?' I could not bring myself to tell him the truth; I could only assure him I was okay. He needed to hear I was fine, which also helped him.

I sat Jamie on my lap, then cuddled him and said it was going to be just him and Mummy for a while, and so it would be his job to look after his mummy. I then tickled him and he giggled. We both laughed and I stopped suddenly, putting on a serious face, so he would pay attention. I said, 'Listen son, from now on darling you must finish all your food so you can be strong enough to take care of Mummy, okay?'

He smiled, and with his tiny voice, replied, 'Okay, Mummy, but is Daddy coming later?'

'*Oh no, Jamie please don't*', I muttered to myself, feeling teary again and then I said something that was unimportant which also translated to being conservative with the truth. To take his mind off it I said, 'Jamie, show Mummy your muscles, let me see how strong you are.' He did, flexing his tiny muscles and even Mum and the driver joined in as we laughed.

The pain was very hard to bear and the fact that I was punishing Jamie as well, made me sad because he loved his dad a great deal and James loved him very much. Jamie is the spitting image of James. I had to stop crying for my son's sake and I tried desperately to think of something harsh in order to be strong.

I had to face the actual situation; the truth, no matter how much I loved James. In doing so, I had to remember why I was leaving him in the first place. He had not behaved appropriately as a good husband and father should to Jamie and I. He took us for granted by never being there for us when we needed him most and always came home late since we were not a priority to him.

This was a short-term sacrifice that had to be made and endured for a long-term gain, I thought. Love does not hurt, but in my case I had been bruised and battered in the name of it. Auntie Flo's words floated back to me afresh at this point and I decided to face reality by genuinely asking myself the question, 'Is a black eye an expression of love? My crime? Love!' The reality check helped to reduce the guilt I felt about what I thought I was doing to Jamie a little bit.

We arrived at the airport at 9.45a.m. due to the rush-hour traffic and Mum asked the driver to wait and take her back home. As she hurriedly helped me with my luggage to the entrance, I gave her a quick hug. She hugged Jamie too and I asked her to hurry back to the waiting driver. This was to prevent the taxi driver from increasing his fare and to avoid prolonging my agony of saying *goodbyes* as I was already missing my precious Mum.

On entering the airport, my eyes scanned through the notices and signs for directions and the appropriate check-in desk, and then I noticed the one for Newark had closed.

As I was pondering over what to do next, a female member of staff asked if I needed any help. I said, *'Yes'*, and told her where we were travelling to. She confirmed that check-in was closed and that I was late. I was aware of the check-in time being two hours before travel, but I was snookered and there was nothing I could have done to get there quicker. Somehow, I just knew a miracle would happen, since I had suffered enough, but I did not know the shape or form it would appear in.

We were late *(not due to African time),* but because I had to work around James, if not, I would have been up at 6.00a.m. to get ready. I explained to the female airport staff member *(who was perhaps either a manager or supervisor)* that I was fleeing from my husband and she was very understanding and sympathetic.

An angel in disguise she certainly was. She stretched out her right hand for our documents and I gave her my passport and our tickets. On checking they were all valid, she asked us to follow her and then quickly grabbed my suitcase to help me as we ran towards security while she was on her walkie-talkie, giving orders.

I struggled to keep up with her, since I was carrying Jamie *(who could not walk fast)* and my hand luggage. We hurried through until we reached security and the lady handed back my documents and suitcase. She was still communicating via the walkie-talkie while we were being checked.

Soon after, a male airport staff member quickly labelled my suitcase and rushed off with it. We then followed closely behind the lady as we made our way through the departure gate until we reached the aircraft. She bid us farewell, then I gave her a big hug, thanked her and located our seats. She was, without a doubt, an angel sent by God to help us as there was no way I would have travelled without her help. God was on our side. God knew my plight and had had mercy on us.

Had I missed the flight, perhaps I would have done something stupid or slept at the airport, but one thing was for sure, I would never have gone back to that house, as James would have buried me alive. I was almost 45 minutes late and God had made the plane wait for us. Due to our rushing and in my panic, I never thought to ask for her name, but to this day I still pray for her and her family.

★ ★ ★

Leaving Mum was heartbreaking and I was devastated. I knew I would miss her very much as she is the one person who truly loves me, apart from Jamie, of course. She is not only my Mum, but also my big sister and my confidante. I knew she would miss me too, so I prayed silently for God to console her, to keep her well and strong, and to look after her for me in my absence.

My heart went out to the rest of my siblings who live in different places, and Dad who was permanently based in Nigeria with his other family. I prayed for God to bless them all, including James. As I stated earlier, *you do not fall out of love overnight,* especially with someone you love truly and deeply.

Although, it was one-sided love, I had tried my best to keep my side of the bargain all along. I prayed for God to comfort him in our absence and to give him the ability to change his ways, so he could be good to his next wife and for Jamie later in life. Now, I had to be strong for my son. I had to think about our safety and our uncertain future, and then I prayed for God to take control.

This mantra kept me sane and strong throughout my darkest days. **'Failure is not fatal, but failure to change might be.'** Everyone makes mistakes and fails, but it is what you do after the mistake or failure that makes all the difference.

★ ★ ★

We arrived safely at LaGuardia Airport Newark and my beautiful cousin Preference, Auntie Florence's eldest daughter, met and took us to their home in New York. We received a hearty welcome from the entire family who had heard our story beforehand and they assured us all would be well. I felt relieved, safe and free from James.

Everything was fine and we settled in well. Auntie Florence and her husband Uncle Pelas did all they could to make Jamie and I comfortable. They counselled me for about two months and were both shocked to see how broken and beaten I was. Thankfully, through their love and support, I felt better and gradually gained some self-confidence. June soon came and it was Jamie's 4th birthday.

We received gifts of balloons and cards delivered to Auntie Florence's house and I was happy. However, when I saw the sender's name, I felt faint as thoughts of James came rushing through my head, *'Oh no, this cannot be happening, am I dreaming? Is this a joke? Mr. Everywhere, the ubiquitous James had found us at last!'* I was scared. The horror and nightmare I had suffered at his hands all came flooding back.

'James has found us.' I said to no one in particular, but to everyone in the house. My self-confidence took a nose-dive. I was frightened to leave my room. The bathroom and kitchen were as far as Jamie and I could go, never venturing out of the house.

Convinced that James was stalking us, I closed the windows and curtains in my room. It made the room dark but I did not dare switch on the light to prevent any reflections in case James was outside watching us. The only source of light in the room was from the television. I was frightened and would not let Jamie out of my sight or play outside due to fear. It was so bad I almost had a panic attack.

Everyone was baffled but tried their best to reassure me that we were safe in the room and that James would have to get through them first to reach either Jamie or me.

I was responsible for his coming to the States because I forgot to give his name to the authorities at the airport as my Aunty had advised. How could I have been so foolish? To be honest, it had totally escaped me, as I did not once think of James when we landed. The distance may have made it a certainty for me and I thought it was impossible for him to come over.

On the third day of the fear-imposed siege, Uncle Pelas decided to take a proper look at the card and found the name of the company that had sent it. He carried out some research, traced where it had come from and how the company had got our address. He later found out that James was not in the US, but instead he had paid a company in the UK that contacted its branch in New York to send the card and balloons.

I was relieved but ashamed that James had driven such pathological fear into me that I was still so scared of him, even when he was thousands of miles away. Fortunately, that was the first and last time he sent anything. Although, the question that kept tugging at my heart was, 'how on earth had James got hold of Auntie Flo's address?'

★ ★ ★

Much later, Mum mentioned that my younger brother Michael had informed her that, as soon as James got home that day, he saw my letter and keys. He had then rushed to my Mum's, but she had not returned from the airport. He showed my letter to Michael who was neither aware of what had happened nor what was going on and then he zoomed past in the car a few minutes afterwards *(which confirmed my earlier assumptions that he had hid the car in order to catch me out).*

James telephoned my sister, Gloria in London. She was also unaware of my secret plan, since I had not told anybody apart from Mum. Gloria never knew about our fights or what I had been through, so when she learnt from James that Jamie and I were in America, she thought we were only visiting. Therefore, James, the devil incarnate seized the opportunity to deceive and trick her into giving him the names and addresses of my closest relations in the US.

To Gloria, Christine and Auntie Florence would most certainly have been the first ones; hence, she innocently supplied James with their addresses. Gloria was not to blame as she never knew anything about my plan to desert James. As far as she was concerned, James was my husband, so why would she not provide him with any information he wanted regarding my relatives in the US?

The plan was to inform my family as soon as I was successfully out of the country, but James, the forever-smooth operator, got to Gloria before Mum returned from the airport and obtained the addresses.

The other mystery was how exactly had Mr. Everywhereness found out we were in New York and not in Florida with my sister Christine? Only God knows, but I think he must have derived his conclusion from my Auntie Florence's visit just three months earlier. Lesson learnt: Tell everyone!

With the issue of how James had located us sorted out, my panic was over and things went back to normal. I made regular phone calls to Mum in England and on one occasion, she informed me that James had failed to pay the rent on the shop and the house as they were both in my name, he had auctioned everything in the shop and had turned my home into a brothel, adding that our neighbours now referred to my house as *the red-light whorehouse.*

The following morning I called my housing officer, Miss Elle to inform her of my absence and she promised to take the necessary action. The next time I phoned her for an update she said she had had great difficulty evicting him as there were so many women living in the house. They had refused to leave peacefully and she had no choice but to involve the police who successfully got them all out.

At some point, the two neighbours on either side of me noticed there were big flies buzzing about and decided to find out the source. They soon discovered that James had a pile of black bin bags in the back garden that were breeding gigantic flies. It was the summer of 1997. Due to our constant fights and because I had vanished without a trace, my neighbours assumed he had killed me, hence they panicked and informed the police.

The police responded promptly, only to find out that the bags contained rubbish that he had stored for several weeks but never bothered to take out for the weekly collections. All of these events were recounted to me by Mum, and confirmed officially by Miss Elle, my housing officer.

Seeing the effect James still had on me regarding the gift palaver, Auntie Florence and Uncle Pelas knew they still had more work to do and they continued to counsel me. In the process, Uncle Pelas got a cassette tape recorder and asked me to speak into it while he recorded. Referring to the Bible, he mentioned that Joseph had to eventually face and confront Pharaoh (his adversary) and he asked me to imagine that James was in front of me. I had to be brave and strong enough to face my fears in order to confront my adversary. In light of the recent information about James, my heart was hardened. As a result, I spoke into the tape recorder and confronted James (my Pharaoh) like never before. Afterwards, I felt better and a lot stronger!

★ ★ ★

My candid answer to the mind-boggling questions, in a nutshell, is simply because I was beyond foolish, crazily blinded by love and hopelessly in love with the ideal of being in love! Lesson learnt: Do not let your heart rule your head, for it is much better to let your head rule your heart!

Everything happens for a reason and now, I can sincerely say that my relationship with James was not a total waste of my time. I truly do not regret my union with him, because it is via that marriage that I had, and still have, my greatest gift in the whole world. My most precious son, Jamie.

★ ★ ★

Six months after I moved to New York, Auntie Florence and her family moved to Connecticut. I was devastated because I had lost a veritable source of courage, support and encouragement. The family had treated us very well, with such great care, and although they all wanted us to move down with them, I did not want to.

I decided that I would need to be on my own one day and it was right that I started at the point when I felt strong enough to look after Jamie and myself. As God is forever faithful, through a family friend, I later found and secured accommodation in Brooklyn, paying only peanuts for a lovely flat.

Even so, things were rough and tough. Getting money was difficult. With my having no legal documents or permit to work, I had to take on small jobs helping my Aunt's friends. Auntie Florence and her family were still trying to help, and my family members in England regularly sent me money for our upkeep.

In November, when I could not bear the hardship any longer, Mum learnt about my predicament and she begged me to return to the United Kingdom. In trying to persuade me, she promised that she and my brothers would protect us from James. At first, I was adamant, saying I would rather live like a pauper in a foreign land than go back to the UK and be killed by James.

'Who would look after Jamie if anything happened to me?' I asked my relations. I had no definite answers or guarantees, but after much persuasion from most of my family, I succumbed. Staying and suffering in the US in a way, meant that James had won by making life miserable for me thousands of miles away. Besides, I realised that I could not run for ever. I had to face and confront my

Pharaoh at some point! My mind was made up and I decided to buy our one-way tickets back home to England in December, just before Christmas.

★ ★ ★

Mum, Max and Michael were at the airport arrivals area waiting and were very glad to see us, although, they hardly recognised me as I had become half of my former self through weight loss.

Given that I had lost everything I owned previously, I had no choice but to move in with my Mum and I quickly set about looking for a job and a home for Jamie and I.

Chapter Twenty:
Post-America Life/Out
With the Old

C oming back from America, I was a changed woman. Love had dealt me a colossal and devastating blow. As a result, I promised myself that I was no longer going to take any nonsense from anyone, let alone James. Out with the old and in with the new. I decided on a completely new outlook on life by re-inventing myself and getting a new chic look to go with it.

Starting at the top, my hair stylist worked her magic by dyeing my hair platinum blonde, finishing it off with a trendy short cut and *sleek s-curl* waves. The result was an elegant and sophisticated cutting-edge look, which boosted my self-confidence enormously. Having shed some pounds *(although, I was not quite as huge as a whale previously)*, I wore only fabulous petite outfits and I felt pretty all over again; like a *glamour-puss*. The icing on the cake was that a friend of mine called Evelyn, wanted me to do some modelling for her. Even though I was flattered, I thanked her but turned her down.

Shortly after, I changed my name to Renée Matthews by deed poll. I derived the name Renée from Irene. It means Reborn in French and I truly am! Matthew is my Dad's first name so all I added was an 's' at the end to make it sound like a surname.

I got Jamie into a good Catholic school and secured a sales job working twelve hours a day, while Mum helped take care of Jamie after school. Two months later, the good Miss Elle allocated me a house of my own. It was a stone's throw from where I used to live with James, however, it was closer to Mum's; on the next block and only four houses away, to be precise.

Feeling lucky, happy and delighted did not come close to describing how I felt. Ecstatic, blessed and highly favoured seemed closer and I was doing cartwheels of joy in my mind.

Working and living with Mum had enabled me to save some money. I was able to hire decorators to paint every nook and cranny of the house, despite it being almost brand new at only eighteen months old. The decorators painted the house in light cream tones and it turned out just the way I wanted it. Next, I chose and bought cream-coloured carpets to match which included free fittings, followed by a double and a single bed for Jamie and I; the only furniture we had.

Our home was bare. We had no other furniture or mod cons *(it was minimalist to the extreme),* but we had all we needed. It was clean and lovely, with chic contemporary soft furnishings from the United States *(the only luxury I could afford while in America).* I was happy and content at that moment in time, but I intended to save some more to buy only brand new things gradually.

Jamie spent most of his time at my Mum's while I was at work and the agreement *(between Jamie and I)* was that he could watch television when he got home from school, but only after his dinner and homework.

Chapter Twenty-One:
The Devil Rears Its Ugly Head...
Again!

J ames mysteriously learnt about our return from the States and had the audacity to rush to Mum's house. Luckily, I was at home that day. Without any pleasantries, he made a big fuss about him having custody of Jamie and threatened to take him from me. *I can deal with a lot but I was done dealing with stupidity.*

I was ready! I was no longer scared of him and I boldly asked him to bring it all on. I was prepared to fight my Pharaoh all the way and I intended to enjoy the ride in the process. Mum and my two strapping brothers, Max and Mike, were also present as they had both returned from work. They wanted to teach James a lesson he would not forget in a hurry, but I asked them to leave him to me. However, seeing his miserable form stunned me.

I was taken aback to see that he had grown a crown of dreadlocks on his head that looked so massive, they resembled tree *trunks*. The pile of locks made his *dread head* seem very huge and his face was barely visible. He was in a wretched and despicable state; a far cry from the sleek, elegantly dressed and devilishly handsome James I once knew. He was a sorry sight and he looked as old as my Granddad.

I did not want to stoop to his level, so I quickly composed myself and attempted to deliver my *(rehearsed tape recorded)* speech in a calm way, to ensure it really sank into his porous brain. It was apparent that my earlier words did not seem to have had any effect on him, so I said, 'Look here, James…' he was still ranting and raving, hence I raised my right hand to silence him.

Full of airs and graces, I spoke as he stared at me in surprise. 'You have no right to come here blabbing as I am done with your *shite*. Now, I am going to warn you just once, so listen carefully. If I *ever* see your miserable self in this area again, I will make sure that is the last thing you *ever* do!'

James was stunned at how I had spoken to him. Well, it made him quieten down somewhat although, he went away, cursing and mumbling the words, 'I'll see you in court', as he left.

James filed for legal custody of Jamie. He was still on income support and could afford to get a solicitor through legal aid. I had no assistance since I was in full-time employment, and moreover, I saw no point in paying a solicitor to tell my story to the judge since there was nothing wrong with either my mouth or memory.

Social Services were involved and I defended myself by referring to records of his numerous arrests at several police stations in London. The records stated the number of times he had assaulted me including extensive reports from Social Services, which contained the incident when he mistakenly hit Jamie in London.

With God on my side and as my solicitor, every piece of information was verified and confirmed. Justice won! The court ruled against him and his case was dismissed and thrown out.

James was asked to buy Jamie occasional gifts, such as for birthdays, Easter celebrations and Christmas etc., and was granted supervised visits through a social worker. Predictably, he only bought a few gifts once and then stopped. That was the last we ever saw or heard of him. Despite the constant persistence of the Child Support Agency for me to claim child maintenance from James, I never did because I loathed his money and anything to do with him.

Chapter Twenty-Two:
'F' Is For ...

I tried to file for divorce as soon as I returned from the States but I had no idea where James was living. Therefore, I paid a Solicitor to locate him in order to serve him with the necessary papers, but James never responded.

As a result, I waited for five years, after which my solicitor was able to apply to the courts to dissolve the marriage on the grounds of a five-year separation with or without his consent. The decree nisi arrived by post, followed by the decree absolute and the marriage between James and I was officially over. F is for final and freedom. I was finally free of James. Forever.

Chapter Twenty-Three:
No Rest For The Wicked

N inety-nine percent of the information in this chapter is based on witness accounts, which took place in my absence and were obtained second-hand. The one percent is therefore for the margin of error and benefit of the doubt. The reliable witnesses were my housing officer Miss Elle, who documented some parts officially, my Mum, who had no reason whatsoever to lie to me, and the Experian records. Most of the information were verified much later and found to be true.

Through Experian *(a provider of credit information)*, I discovered that James had applied for numerous loans in my name. Fortunately for me, most were rejected, and on my return, the necessary steps were taken to clear my identity *(being a victim of identity theft and fraud according to the subject's rights, under the Data Protection Act 1998)*. I was glad to be rid of him and his name, but my other personal details remain the same.

After I left James, I learnt he began living his life as he pleased. *Fair enough!* That did not mean he was restricted or on a leash while we were together *(since he was hardly ever at home and was usually up to no good)*. Whilst I was around, his shenanigans were limited, to a certain extent, in the sense that he, at least returned home to me *(well, most times)*, no matter how late. He was, however, smart enough to know that if he did not *(although I never had to)*, I would waste no time in reporting him missing if he had stayed out for more than one day.

I never had many friends, but I found out that he had slept with most of them. A young girl who was in a junior class at school *(Idia College, Nigeria)* often visited us in London and helped to babysit Jamie a couple of times. It never occurred to me at the time that she was also taking care of James's sexual needs.

James was a *deviously* clever man; he made sure I never caught him with other women, or so he thought. I truly do not remember seeing him with other women *(even if I did, I deceived myself anyway)*, but I knew, because my instincts were so strong, I could visibly see it. A woman gets to know and can sense if her man is two-timing.

On the other hand, no matter how strong my instincts were, I was weak and could do nothing about it. What's more, I never failed to carry out my matrimonial duty, even when he stank of booze and weed; regardless of how revoltingly sick I felt or how much I cringed. He was my husband, how could I refuse him? We made love in the very early hours of the morning I left him *(although it felt like I was kissing or making love to the devil)*.

Thankfully, with the help of Aunty Flo, I am glad I was strong enough to finally follow my instincts, hence my last letter to him ended with the words: *'I love you honey, but not enough to die for you.'* I did not want any *unwanted gifts* such as AIDS or any venereal diseases from him, which was another reason I left him. It was rumoured that one of his closest friends *(God rest his soul)* had died from the disease. The physical abuse was secondary; a normal occurrence, and I was already used to it.

In my opinion, James was not sad or remorseful that I had left him, but because he missed his son a lot. Perhaps, what hurt him the most was that his pride and over-inflated ego had been wounded and trampled on. I am sure he could not bring himself to accept the fact that I had fled from him with our son. Knowing James, he would have felt much better and happier if it were the other way round. Worst still, his *fool* was unavailable to massage or nurse his bruised ego back to how colossal it once was.

The lowdown was that James quickly recovered from the initial shock of our disappearance and he gave up shortly after a few unsuccessful attempts to track us down. He then auctioned away the remaining stock left in the shop and closed it down. Afterwards, he became as free as a bird and turned the house into a brothel. In the midst of *wakibaki, booze,* and *hoochie mamas* galore, he was dubbed the *dread lord* of weed, drank like a fish, played music full-blast all day long and partied as he pleased.

'He was on a spree of self-destruction', I was reliably informed. Only God knew what kind of activities took place in what was once our humble abode turned *harem.* With great dreadlocks as thick as *tree trunks* that practically touched his waist, it was shocking to the system to see James, who was usually perfectly dressed, like that.

I learnt that most of my neighbours referred to James as a menace to the neighbourhood, as well as to society. *His dad would turn in his grave if he could see him!* Almost everyone I knew who also knew James, talked about this particular girlfriend or possibly, *Baby mama* of his, nicknamed *Hightower*. They said she had such a high ponytail on her head that, when she drove in her car, it was all they could see poking out of the sunroof when it was open. With his timber-like dreadlocks, they must have complimented each other.

In every rumour, there is always an element of truth. I saw the massive dreadlocks on his head with my very own eyes on our return from America.

After my housing officer had successfully evicted James and his cohorts, he rented a flat that was paid for by housing benefit since he was still receiving income support. While he was strung out on a *weed/booze* binge one day, he set his flat on fire and had the effrontery to ask my younger sister, Geraldine, to let him move into her spare room.

How dare he? Would any sane person do that? I had already left him, all ties had been severed and he was no longer our problem. Where were his numerous girlfriends to help him out?

Of course, Geraldine turned down his request and was relieved when she later heard he had moved in with one of his girlfriends *(not Hightower)*.

Chapter Twenty-Four:
Second Chance – A Fresh Start With Mr. Right.

In March 1998, I met Tom, a sweet, caring, handsome and dark-haired gentleman, at work. Originally from Glossop, Derbyshire, he is extremely witty, has a wonderful sense of humour and is always great fun to be around. Before long, we became very good friends and he treated me like a lady, even though he was my boss.

Being a very private person, I love to keep myself to myself, but I often engaged in some chats with a few of my colleagues during our coffee breaks. At some point during our chats, I often dropped little hints and gave everyone in my office the impression that I had a boyfriend back in America, to shake guys off my tail.

One day, Tom gave me a lift home when my car broke down and as we got to Mum's, Jamie was playing football outside. I wanted Mum to thank Tom for fetching me home and as Tom was getting out of the car to say a quick hello to Mum, Jamie passed the ball over to him and they ended up playing football for about 30 minutes. During that time, Jamie had asked Tom for his name, introduced himself *(at only four years old)* and he took to Tom straight away. It seemed like they had known each other for a long time. Exhausted, Tom finally went inside to say hello to Mum, had a quick cup of coffee and then drove off home.

A few weeks later, while having lunch with Tom during our break, we chatted, and I revealed the truth about having a *boyfriend* in America.

'It was necessary for me to tell a fib to scare men away since I have only just recovered from a very abusive relationship', I confided in him. 'Men are evil.' I said.

Tom was very sorry to hear it, but he too revealed to me that he had also left a bad marriage behind and he intended to relocate to Ireland the following week for a fresh start.

'Not all men are the same, you know.' Tom said.

'Hmm', I said.

Then suddenly, he said, 'We are two good people, why don't we just be together?'

I was shocked and very surprised as I was not expecting him to say that. Although I had recently transformed myself, I had tried to avoid attracting any attention by dressing down. I had bought myself a long black coat that covered most of my body and I went to work every day dressed like an old woman to put men off. How could he like or fancy a woman with a lengthy coat and very short hair? I thought he was joking and laughed it off, but he told me that he had never been more serious about anything.

'Tom, we are friends. Please let's leave it at that because another relationship is the last thing on my mind now.' I said, keen for him to drop the matter.

'Please think about it.'

'Okay', I said, just to shut him up, but without taking him seriously.

I jokingly recounted the conversation I had had with Tom to my Mum when I got home, as I had promised never to hide anything from her again *(especially after everything that had happened with James)*. I expressed my fear of men due to what I had been through in the past, but she advised me by saying that not all men were like James or my Dad.

Mum said Tom seemed like a decent man and that I should try being with him. I mentioned that I had never dated an English man before, to which she replied, 'Are they not humans? We are all the same beings, at least give him a chance. What have you got to lose?' *There goes Mum again, firing away her questions per minute.*

However, I know she means well. She spoke firmly and her lovely eyes were filled with love and affection as she tried to make me see reason. Mum continued, 'If it works out, fine and if it doesn't, then you move on. One thing I know for sure, my dear daughter is', Mum said pausing to swallow some saliva, 'If you don't try, you'll never know, so please, you must never let a good man pass you by.'

Those were the kind and wise words of my best friend and sweet Mother. *Twist of fate!* I had to beg her to accept James then, and now, she was doing the same by talking me into *giving Tom a chance.* Who ever came up with *Mums know best?* To me, they are absolutely correct. *What had she said about James? How had he turned out? Where was he now? I rest my case!*

I asked Tom for some more time to think about it and he said he was a patient man and that he would wait. The only little problem, as he reminded me, was that I should consider the fact that he was leaving for Ireland. Tom promised to wipe away the tears from my past years, to look after me and that he would willingly give me all he had. *Then, wait for this!* Tom said Jamie would be number one in our household.

Jamie, number one? Those were the magic words. I was sold! Instead of moving to Ireland, he moved in with Jamie and I, a week later and together, we made our home.

We had both had very promiscuous ex-partners, so, I wanted to start my life with Tom afresh and with a clean bill of sexual health. This meant that we had to be celibate for three months.

'Three whole months?' Tom repeated, he could not believe his ears. 'This is unbelievable, but why?' he asked, struggling to get over the initial shock.

'Yes, darling', I replied, and I carefully explained my reason, which was the fact that our ex-partners were very promiscuous. I told him that I wanted both of us to be tested for HIV and other venereal diseases, to find out if we had been affected or not. Three months of abstinence it had to be, because if there was any infection, it might take a minimum of three months to show up in our systems. *I hadn't been with anyone since James but I wasn't sure about Tom.*

'I am an old-fashioned girl' I admitted to Tom, 'I take my body and my relationships seriously. My body is the temple of God. When I am with you, it is going to be with you and no one else, therefore, should I catch anything, I will know that it is from you sweetheart, and vice versa.'

Tom looked worried and perplexed. I knew I had to explain further.

'Darling, don't take it the wrong way. Please bear with me and try to understand. I know it's going to be very difficult, but when we are both clear, we'll be totally free with each other.'

'Sweetheart, if that's what you want, then that's exactly what we'll do.' Tom said, lovingly. 'Although, it is going to be hard since you are so beautiful, but anything for you babe, and, yes, I do understand.'

That was my angel's reply. Is it any wonder I love him so much? It was very difficult indeed for us both. We often had to try very hard to resist one another although we did everything else apart from have sex. Those three months were the longest ever and they seemed to last for a year, but when our results came back negative, our celebration was pure and absolute bliss.

After our celibacy period ended, Tom confessed to me that it was the hardest thing he had ever done in his entire life. Taking my hands in his, he led me to the sofa and we sat down next to each other. Tom said, 'My darling, my darling, please listen to me', looking lovingly into my eyes. 'You were absolutely correct. I never knew it then, but I now know that we have done what was best, as we are now completely free with each other.'

He continued, 'You are an exceptionally clever girl with high morals, beauty and brains to have come up with such a difficult, but extremely rewarding idea. You can never really put a price on peace of mind; no stress, ifs or buts and I have only the utmost respect for you, my darling.'

'Wow! Thanks babes. You see, I told you we would be much happier', I said, smiling and glad that we had been through the worst, to come up better lovers and best friends.

'It will go down in history that you are the only woman who has and will ever do that to me, my Queen. Never again!'

He went on to say that he only agreed just to make me happy since it was what I wanted. Tom actually thought I would crack and would not last and therefore, he stated, 'Little did I know you were one hard-faced *biatch,* my love', smiling and saying it in the nicest, *sexiest* possible way that he could make that word sound.

I smiled, batting my long eyelashes and pouting my full luscious lips in a way that I was certain would make him weak at the knees. As he pulled me closer to him, hugging me lovingly, I managed to wriggle out of his warm embrace knowing what was next. However, when this fine figure of a man caught and held me close, I became putty in his hands. I could not resist him.

★ ★ ★

We were free to get married after the divorces from our previous partners and we happily set a date for our wedding. Our traditional marriage *(Native Law & Custom)* date was set for September 19, 2003 and the venue was at my Mum's house. Dad arrived from Nigeria a couple of days before our wedding, to give me away and to walk me down the aisle a second time.

My parents hail from Edo state in Nigeria but are from different local communities. Dad comes from a village called Oza-nisi Aibiokunla in Orhionmwon Local Government while Mum is a native of Odighi in Ovia Local Government.

A Native Law & Custom or Customary Law Marriage is the recognised and most important part of a marriage in Edo state. The indigenes of the land are known as the *Binis* or the *Edos* and the dialect is the Edo or Bini language.

The term *dowry* is similar to the *bride price* or *purchase price,* and the soon-to-be husband refers to it as a payment in the form of gifts, money, cowries or the total sums or fees. The dowry is a very important part of a valid Customary Law Marriage in Nigeria. It is used to seal the marriage agreement between the two parties and their families.

In the olden days, a bride price took the form of labour carried out by the suitor into consideration for the parents of his wife-to-be. In addition to the labour, a small cash payment and drinks were also required. Nowadays, it is easier to pay the bride price in the form of cash *or in some cases, even by Visa, Master or Platinum card.*

The idea behind the payment of a fee, however, does not indicate that one has *bought* a wife or that she is a *prized possession*. It simply symbolises that she is given to the suitor on loan, and in the event that she is treated badly, or refuses to continue with the marriage, she would be returned to her parents and the *dowry* or *payment* would be returned.

★ ★ ★

On Friday evening, September 12, 2003, Tom's friends and brothers all went over to Leek, a small market town in the county of Staffordshire, to celebrate his stag night in the pub that belonged to Tom's brother, Carl. As the landlord, he hosted the evening for Tom and his friends for free as his wedding gift.

While Tom and his gang went to Leek, one of my friends organised a hen party for me at her house. She invited a few close friends, including my family, and some brought with them various tasty dishes and drinks. That night we all ate, drank, danced, told many good tales and had great fun.

Two days before Our Native Law & Custom ceremony, Uncle Pelas, Aunt Florence, Preference and Belief *(their children)* all came from the States. Auntie Pat and her family had arrived from London the day before. I was so excited. We never bothered with and simply omitted the traditional marriage section with James, which may have been the reason it did not *last.*

On the morning of September 19, Tom, Jamie and I arrived early to help at Mum's house. Gezza, Max and Mike were already there since they lived in the neighbourhood. Gloria, Segun and their three kids, Michelle and Mum's two sisters; Auntie Mercy and Auntie Felicia including their families had also come from London. Christine and her family could not make it from Florida due to the 9/11 pandemonium, but sent their love and best wishes.

The whole place and atmosphere was buzzing; there was excitement in the air as we prepared, arranged and decorated. A few of Mum's friends and relatives helped to cook a variety of delicious African dishes and there was an assortment of drinks available. Everything was arranged before 5.00p.m. and Tom's family were the first to arrive.

The ceremony began at 7.00p.m. after most of our guests arrived *African time*, and the oldest member of my family said a prayer to start off the ceremony. Afterwards, the coconuts and kola nuts *(Nigeria's seed of togetherness)*, brought specially by Dad from Nigeria were broken, cut into pieces and shared among the guests. The kola nut is a simple nut that is grown in Nigeria. It symbolises long life and it is traditionally used at a variety of events as a sign of friendship, hospitality and respect.

Dressed in a luxurious velvety black, gold and red damask wrapper called an *igbegbe,* and a blouse festooned with thousands of tiny coral coloured beads, I felt like a king's queen with royal headgear to match. Tom wore a complete set of white kaftan with a long set of beads around his neck. He looked smashing, but for an ex-soldier he was stunned and petrified when four pretty damsels came out and paraded past him. They were all petite in size, dressed as brides, fully covered by thick veils and carefully chosen to look as convincing as possible to the groom and our guests.

The general idea was to confuse the groom whose task it was to choose his true bride from amongst the others. Tom was bamboozled with all the goings-on because the lasses were almost identical. He chose bride number four and chose wrong! Tom had made a *blunder* and had committed a crime called *wrongitism* in *Government's* dictionary! A mistake that is punishable and at the discretion of the father-of-the-bride *(knowing Government, flogging could not have been more appropriate, despite him being older now).*

'Oh no', Tom said, 'wrong one, sorry.' Everybody in the room fell silent. They were all poker-faced. Just then, I started to walk across the room towards him and he nervously took a quick peek by slightly lifting up my veil to ensure he was correct.

Completely certain, he unveiled and hugged me, then everyone present stood up and clapped for Tom with huge smiles on their faces. He had been brave, but very glad, even though he later confessed to me that it had been worse than his army drilling. He also stated that, although he loved every minute of it, he did not fancy going through it again. *My angel had got the whole point!*

It was so very humorous and all part of the process required to make the ceremony more lively. Following that, my Dad, uncles and some other guests said a few more prayers for us and then the food was served.

When it was time for the bride price/dowry to be paid, Gezza stood in front of Tom, holding a silver box in her hands and he obediently placed the money he had on him, all £252.57 British pounds and pence into the box. When asked for some more, Tom checked again and then turned his pockets inside out to prove he had nothing more left to give.

Jokingly, Dad said, 'Tom, you have to pay for choosing wrongly, *remember?' Government* did not intend to let him forget or get off lightly by asking him to write a promissory note, stating, 'I promise to pay the sum of £500 for my wife' *(we still have the note in our possession to date. Had Tom met Government 30 years ago, being an ex-soldier might not have exempted him from Dad's floggings).* Just kidding, for Tom is a good man and deserves none of that *(but James certainly did).*

We often joke about the fact that he still owes my Dad, and although Tom has offered to pay him more than ten times since then, Dad always said, 'Oh no, don't you worry about it yet, *but,* you still owe me.'

Following the dowry payment, everyone stood up to welcome Tom and his relatives into the family. The merriment carried on and then, it was joke-telling time on the agenda. Segun was present, but had his hands full with his two younger children aged two and three *(their first child Trevor, is the same age as Jamie),* while Gloria was busy serving the guests. This time Cousin Billy stood up to introduce himself.

After his greetings, he proceeded to narrate a dialogue between a young man and his father-in-law to be, which is as follows:

Father-in-law: 'Young man, you are coming to seek my daughter's hand in marriage and you are chewing gum? That is a sign of disrespect!'

Young man: 'Sir, I only chew gum when I drink or smoke.'

Father-in-law: 'You mean you drink and smoke, and you are here to seek my daughter's hand in marriage?'

Young man: 'Sir, I only drink and smoke when I go clubbing.'

Father-in-law: 'You go clubbing too?'

Young man: 'I'm sorry sir; I started clubbing when I came out of prison.'

Father-in-law: 'You have also been in prison?' You are an ex-convict. Oh my God!'

Young man: 'Sorry sir, I went to jail when I killed somebody.'

Father-in-law: 'What! You are a killer?'

Young man: 'Sir, it happened out of anger. It was a certain man that did not allow me to marry his daughter so I killed him.'

Father-in-law: 'Oh, you are highly welcome my son. You are on the right track and you are absolutely the right man for my daughter.'

'Have a wonderful evening everyone.' Billy finished, amidst loud sounds of laughter from all present.

Dad smiled at Tom and quickly added, 'Hello Tom, my charming Tom, are you enjoying yourself? I hope you are happy and comfortable.'

Tom nodded and said, 'Yes Daddy', looking a bit puzzled.

Then on a more serious note, followed by *the* look, *Government's look*, Dad said, 'Billy is not referring to you, I hope son? Are you a killer? Speak up now please!' Everyone laughed, including Tom and then, Dad too, eventually.

'No sir, at least not yet sir', Tom replied, 'however sir, it depends on whether or not you are going to give me your daughter, as the ceremony has not yet ended sir. It would also be a good idea for you to remember sir, that I am an ex-soldier sir, for we always answered sir, *sir,* and I was once a sharp shooter sir.' *That sure did wipe the smile off Government's face and I bet it got him thinking.*

That's my witty and hilarious Tom. Always on the ball, although, one has to be thick-skinned or become offended. In my 15 years with him, I have never known anyone to get one over him *yet.* He gives as good as he gets; if not better and he laughs all the way through, shakes it off and nothing ever gets to him. For the life of me, I do not know how he does it. All I need to ask him when we wake up in the morning is, 'Good morning darling, how did you sleep?'

'Lying down.' Tom always answers, smiling. Plain and simple.

To this day, Tom and Mike, my brother, enjoy good-natured banter with one another and there is even sometimes a bit of banter between Tom and my big sister Christine, too. They are all as bad as one another and I often have to step in to put an end to it, because none of them would give in to the others first.

Tom loves to tell jokes and he makes me laugh all the time. *Our motto is; it's easier to smile than to frown, as laughter is the best medicine.* Tom couldn't hurt a fly, but he is very clever and sharp with his tongue, especially when telling humorous jokes. Personally, I have had to develop a thick skin against his idiomatic expressions, but I have also learnt a lot more about humour and wittiness from him too.

After the jokes, Maxwell the house DJ played some music while we all danced until the party finally ended. It was truly awesome. Afterwards, everyone went home to prepare for the next day, the big day. Our wedding day.

★ ★ ★

On the morning of September 20, 2003, I woke up early, got dressed and hurried out of the house to attend my 8.00a.m. hair appointment. Hair done, I rushed back home to find my friend and makeup artist Judith, waiting for me. Judith did her best and I was happy.

Susie, my maid of honour, also one of my best friends, is a lovely Oriental beauty who has really been a true friend indeed. She arrived shortly after Judith, followed by the bridesmaids: my sisters Michelle and Gezza, Suzan my Goddaughter, a friend called Charlotte, and my five flower girls. Tom had Jamie, Max, Mike, his two brothers Dave and Carl, then Dale, his best friend of over 40 years, and two others, as his groomsmen.

Our wedding was at 11.00a.m. While I was busy getting ready with my bridal damsels, the last thing Tom called out to say to me *(as I did not let him see me),* was, 'My darling, please don't be late.' I promised not to. However, due to all the last minute preparations, I could not help it and I was almost two hours late.

Our guests travelled from far and wide and while they were waiting, some friends joked and teased Tom, saying that I would not turn up, but Tom was steadfast.

We finally made it to Manchester Cathedral in a beautifully decorated cream stretch limo. I got out of the car, and as if I was not late enough, my camera crew surrounded me, snapping shots *paparazzi style.* I felt like a superstar in my chic Chanel ivory wedding gown that was all mine. *I could not afford to tempt fate by borrowing again.*

Dad was waiting for me. I could sense his *look* coming, so I literally dragged myself into the cathedral and away from the photographers. All eyes were on me and I loved every minute of the attention, as Dad walked me down the aisle. It was simply phenomenal!

Tom was waiting at the altar and as I approached him, he winked at me *(I was happy. He'd forgiven me, I thought).* I smiled at him as Dad put my hand in Tom's hand *(as the Vicar had instructed),* and then walked back to take a seat.

The Officiate cleared his throat, welcomed everybody and then announced, 'If any of you would like to buy Renée a gift, please buy her a watch or clock', and hysterical laughter filled the building as the ceremony started.

It was a particularly beautiful ceremony as we had Jamie beside us all the way through. At just 10 years old, he stood up in the pulpit to read a sermon about a good marriage and he was also the ring bearer. Thereafter, our wonderful Vicar blessed the three of us together as a family before God.

It was a very grand occasion with close to a thousand guests. Auntie Pat was the Master of Ceremonies. During our wedding reception, we danced to our favourite songs *(Wonder of You* by Elvis Presley and *The Best Years of My Life* by Diana Ross), as our special and loving guests watched. What's more, we had a live-band from London. The next day being Sunday, we went back to the cathedral again with our friends and families for a special thanksgiving service.

★ ★ ★

Coincidentally, as a young lass growing up, my dream and prayers included marrying a man who is exactly five years older than I am, one day. I had no idea why, but I met Tom when I was 30 years old and Tom was 35 *(I only knew his age after we had already become an item).* This is the Lord's doing, for He has fulfilled my dream by providing the exact age gap and a man who will truly love me.

Love has hurt and love has healed me! I seldom have occasional nightmares about James in my sleep, but I pinch myself to bring me back to reality as it all belongs in the past now. My marriage to Tom has made me believe in love again and I pray for God to bless him every day.

On the 1st of December 2009, Tom, Jamie and I, went to Benin City, Edo State, Nigeria for the burial of my maternal granddad; the Late Pa Josiah Erhabor, who died at the age of 110 years. During our visit, I showed them several places of interest and took them down *my* memory lane *(including Idia College).*

Tom has given me only reasons to smile and I adore him. We squabble just like every other couple, but we never go to bed angry. We are not perfect but we are perfect for each other. We do know what it takes to have a good and healthy marriage and we respect, love, understand, and try not to take one another for granted.

My angel has worked all his life and has never been on income support in the whole of his 50 years. True to his word, Tom continues to give me everything he has, he treats me like an angel and he calls me his Queen.

He loves and regards Jamie as the son he always wanted, for he already has two daughters from his previous marriage. Tom is always very interested in Jamie's football career and never misses a single match when Jamie is playing, come rain or shine. It is no wonder Jamie calls him *Top of the Pops.*

We are extremely happy and very much besotted with each other. Tom is my true love, my crown and my angel on earth. Fifteen years now and we are still going strong.

Tom, I will always love you. Thank you for giving me the best years of my life.

Chapter Twenty-Five:
Jamie

Jamie, now 19 years old is a very pleasant, respectable and hard-working young man. He is not only bright, but also very driven, and he possesses a very likeable character. However, he sometimes thinks he knows it all and is occasionally, quite a cheeky chap.

I sincerely do believe that he has inherited most of my few good qualities, for he is sociable, trustworthy and reliable. Jamie also has the most wonderful smile that could melt any heart.

No one would ever believe Jamie was born as early as twenty-seven weeks because he is a big, muscular and strapping lad. As a keep fit fanatic who trains at the gym almost every day, he seems so massive and tall to me that I often feel like grabbing a ladder just to reach or hug him.

A keen footballer since the age of three, Jamie is incredibly dedicated, has a remarkable work ethic and makes the most of every opportunity he gets. While playing for a local football club at the age of eight, he featured in a McDonald's advertisement. As a result, his photograph served as a paper tray in all the McDonald's food outlets throughout the United Kingdom.

At the age of 16, he took part in a football competition called Football's Next Star, which aired on Sky Television 2009. Jamie reached the top 20 out of 7,000 contestants in the United Kingdom and Ireland. Unfortunately, due a severe knee injury, he was unable to continue in the competition.

Jamie was later offered a place with Chicago Fire Juniors Youth Soccer Team. Whilst there, I gave him the shock of his life when I travelled all the way to Chicago to surprise him on his 18th birthday. God granted his greatest wish, he had said when he saw me. Since his return, he works part-time and plays football professionally three times a week. Jamie also intends to go to university.

Having taught him from an early age about the ills of smoking and drinking, his fitness regime *(and being a sportsperson),* collectively made it easy for both of us. Thankfully, he has never touched alcohol or smoked in his life.

His number one fan, his Grandma *(my Mum)* gives him a gigantic 180% for his sense of commitment and conscientiousness in everything he does.

One of the things I had feared the most about taking any action against James was the idea of bringing up a child as a single mum. It was partially the reason why I was worried, as I fled to the United States for refuge and sanity.

Happily, I feel proud now, seeing all that Jamie is becoming in life and it is a source of joy for me to watch him grow into a fine man every day. Now I can look back and say with all conviction that nothing should make anyone remain a prisoner in his or her marriage.

With God on your side and the support of family, good friends or the many agencies available, you can live and succeed outside a hellish marriage, be it husband-imposed or in-law generated. Jamie is a credit to his entire family and we are extremely proud of him.

My only regret was the fact that Jamie remembered quite a bit of the abuse I suffered from James, which I never knew about until Social Services interviewed Jamie. I had tried to hide the abuse from him, but it was very difficult as James often hit me in his presence.

I foolishly assumed that a child only begins to develop a retentive memory from the age of five. Never did I realise that it could be from as early as three years old or even younger. I was shocked and it upset me a great deal when I read the social worker's extensive report on the matter.

The one redeeming feature is that it happened so long ago and I honestly pray it has erased from his memory completely. I recently asked Jamie about it and in his own words he said, 'I do not remember anything Mum and I'm really glad I do not.'

'Are you sure son, nothing at all?' I asked again, though, silently thanking God.

'Positive!' Jamie said.

That was all I needed to hear. Yet, I still blame myself for ever letting him witness any form of abuse at that stage in his life and for how he must have felt at the time. Fortunately, it is all over now.

Post-James, Jamie has only ever witnessed love, not abuse from any member of our family or from me. I am indeed positive that he will grow up to model his life after the good, modern and responsible men in our family.

Reading this book, when it is finally finished, will enlighten Jamie. Now as an adult, he will be in a better position to understand and handle it all. This is the main reason I have purposely waited until now to write this book and I will be there for him every step of the way.

Black & White – 'A Survivor's Story' is Jamie's legacy.

My son Jamie, my precious gift, my hero, my angel, my star, the one whom I am blessed with, I thank God for your life. I loved you even before I met you and I am proud of the young man you have become. Thank you for making me a fulfilled mother and the proudest Mum. God bless you son. I love you.

Chapter Twenty-Six: Welcome To Karma Café. No Menus, But You Are Only Served What You Deserve!

F riends who heard about my story often asked why I did not have James repatriated back to Nigeria in the early days of our marriage rather than run away to another country. They were disgusted and thought that I should have sent him packing as soon as I noticed the earliest warning signs or his tendencies towards being an abusive and wife-battering husband.

My answer was, and still is, that I never intended to repay bad with evil, nor did I want to soil my clean hands. Personally, I believe that vengeance is a lazy form of grief, hence, I looked up to the Lord and had cried and prayed for Him to fight my battle; to vindicate and avenge for me. Fortunately, God heard my cry and answered my prayers because James did eventually get his comeuppance.

Years later, a distant relative of James's told me she had seen him and he had told her that *'he was tired of this effing country and was checking out.'* A few weeks later, she said he had actually packed the few belongings he had, and he went back to Nigeria. *'Satan's gone back to hell',* I thought!

Nonetheless, when he ran out of money after staying there for two years, he called to tell her that he had decided to return, and she wished him a safe journey. Unfortunately for him, and fortunately for me, there was the tiny weenie problem of his overstay. As a result, the penalty for overstaying in Nigeria was the refusal of his entry into the UK. *A strange quirk of fate!*

As far as I am concerned, James, at that point, had visited the karma cafe and he had been served *absobloodylutely* what he deserved. He overstayed in Nigeria for more than two years and he can never return to the United Kingdom, according to the terms and conditions of his indefinite leave to remain in the UK. Einstein was not patient or smart enough to have kept up his pretend love in order to apply for his own British passport before I left him.

During the seven years I stayed with James, he got his indefinite stay within the first two years of his arrival in the UK. After receiving his residency permit, Mr. Mugu thought that the sky was the limit *(after which he started to show his true colours).* Had he been as smart as he claimed, he would have applied for his British Citizenship when I advised him to. He kept putting it off, thinking he had all the time in the world. Well, God works in mysterious ways, for He alone knows the reason James was not

EDOS in DIASPORA FOR GOOD GOVERNANCE in NIGERIA (EDGGN).

As a survivor, I am an active and dedicated member of the Women's Aid Federation UK *(a charity organisation for domestic violence against women and children)*. Having been through similar experiences, I understand and empathise with people going through comparable events.

I have written this book to inspire those going through any form of domestic violence or abuse. My message as a survivor is one of hope, to enable other victims to know that there is help and light at the end of the tunnel, when they finally decide that 'ENOUGH IS ENOUGH!'

Writing this book has been very therapeutic for me. 'There is no greater agony than bearing an untold story inside you.' ~Dr. Maya Angelou

Getting the events out of my head and onto paper, has helped me process that very difficult time in my life and it has enabled me to have closure. I now feel a great deal better, extremely elated and incredibly blessed to have the gift of life, love and freedom.

God wrote my story, but I wrote the book, and I hope and pray that many lives will be touched and changed after reading this Book.

Just like the Good Book says: The glory of the latter shall be greater than the former, amen. I am fulfilling God's plan in my life and living my dream. Lord, I thank You for second chances.

Enough Is Enough

Enough is enough is indeed the first step in deciding to change your situation for the better, after recognising the early warning signs. *'One swats a fly only if it annoys that person' (Cypriot proverb).* You have to make the decision to SAY NO TO ANY FORM OF ABUSE, be it emotional, physical or mental. Do not suffer in silence. If it feels wrong, you may be right.

The next step is to make informed decisions, which usually comes from seeking help from family, friends or the appropriate agencies. Taking necessary action by safely walking out of a situation, if possible, is advisable, as enduring abuse could be dangerous or fatal.

Never be bullied into silence. Never allow yourself to be a victim. Accept no one's definition of your life. Define yourself. *~Julia Turner*

No one deserves to be abused mentally, physically or emotionally by another fellow human being. A *black eye* has NEVER been an expression of love and there is no greater feeling than knowing that if he loved you, he would NEVER scare you! Love is giving someone the power to destroy you, but trusting him or her not to. You must never allow anyone to control your emotions, for anyone who controls your emotions rules you, and you will remain a slave to him or her forever.

There is nothing more attractive than a woman who carries herself like a queen and wears her confidence like a crown! Royalty or not, dignity and respect are every woman's birthright!' ~Khari Toure

You, yes you! The one reading this, remember this and use it as a mantra:

There is only one you, for you are awesome, beautiful, strong and amazing. You are God's special being and you, sincerely, are the best at being you!

Forward ever,
Backward never!

Why The Title Black And White?

At the risk of stating the obvious, the title Black & White represents something more deeper and substantial than colour. It represents love between two people from a very different race and background and the ability to appreciate their differences.

'Black & White' illustrates the themes of *'the same but different'*. It establishes that although we are from different parts of the world, with different ethnicities, race groups, different attitudes, behavioural patterns and personalities, it does not change the fact that we are all one; human beings. Beings of love.

The ability to love is what makes us all human as nature intended and we are all capable of loving one another in spite of our obvious differences. Love knows neither language, barrier or colour. Everyone should be free to love; love is universal, love is free, love is cosmic and love is all around us.

Love is the greatest, most powerful force in the universe. It's a treasure that people would give anything for, yet it costs nothing to give or to receive. There is an endless supply, and it can be extended to family, friends and strangers. It increases positivity, and acts like a soul shield against negativity from the outside world. It forgives, trusts, encourages, inspires and makes all who have it into better people. It is the truth, the path, and the way. Love: Give it, receive it and believe in it ~*Doe Zantamata*

My point in all this is that mutual respect, compatibility, love and understanding, regardless of colour, is important in any relationship - the key to a good one.

Appreciating our differences makes us unique, free and able to love one another. Due to civilisation, it is easier to mix with people from different parts of the world as anything is possible when the heart is released from the chains of ignorance. *'I am glad my parents travelled this far from Nigeria, otherwise, I might never have met my husband Tom!'*

Loving a person and having that person love you back unconditionally, whether Black or White, is the most wonderful and amazing thing in the world. This is what I have found with Tom.

Tom & Renée

Jamie

Self-Help Guide On Domestic Violence & Abuse

Domestic Violence & Abuse: A Hidden Epidemic

An abusive marriage or relationship consists of a victim and an abuser.

A victim is a person or thing that suffers harm or death from another.

An abuser refers to someone who habitually or consistently abuses someone or something.

The sad fact is that almost everyone is likely to experience some form of domestic abuse or violence at some stage or point in his or her life, regardless of who he or she is. Either of them may be the abuser, the victim, the survivor, or may know someone who is going through abuse.

Domestic abuse or violence is a class-leveller. It does not discriminate and it can happen to anyone from different ethnic or social backgrounds, as well as be perpetuated by anybody in any age group, despite their economic or financial status.

Both men and women carry out domestic abuse or violence against one another, although, there are a lot more female victims than males. Most heterosexual marriages, partnerships or same-sex relationships experience domestic abuse. However, the abuse is often lower in same-sex relationships.

It is estimated that one in four women will be a victim of domestic violence in their lifetime. *(The ratio is often higher on a number of occasions)*. One incident of domestic violence is reported to the police every minute. Two women are killed every week in England and Wales by a current or former partner (Homicide statistics, 1998, obtained from *refuge.org.uk*).

Hypothetically, it seems there have been a lot more spouses killed by their partners than the number of soldiers killed in Iraq in the previous years.

The following fact is quoted from Dr. Phil McGraw (USA), on Emotional Abuse: The Victim and Abuser, http://www.drphil.com/articles/article/19/

"The Abuser: Dr. Phil defines an abuser as both a coward and a bully. You choose to abuse where it is safe, in a place where you feel loved and protected. Would you do it in the workplace where you might get fired or in a social situation where others might get insulted?

The Victim: Take responsibility. You have played a role in setting up the relationship this way and you must play a role in changing it. Telling your partner that the treatment is unacceptable is not enough. Your actions speak louder than words, so you need to make two bold moves: Change your own routine or behaviour and tell your partner you will no longer take the abuse.

Dr. Phil refers to a saying: There are no victims, only volunteers. Don't go along to get along. Peace at any price is no peace at all."

Women are more vulnerable and more commonly the victims of abuse. However, domestic violence is not a gender-specific reality; it is unbiased as some women are just as capable as inflicting pain too. Some men do experience abuse from either their female or male partners, but only a few cases become known since they are often too ashamed to report it.

There are also several unreported cases of domestic abuse and violence. The bottom line, however, is that abusive behaviour is unacceptable, regardless of who is giving out the abuse, be it a man, woman, teenager, or an elderly person. Everyone deserves the right to be respected, to feel valued and to be safe.

The following are various forms of domestic abuse and violence:
- Domestic abuse
- Domestic violence or physical abuse
- Financial abuse or economic abuse
- Stalking
- Cyber stalking
- Sexual abuse
- Spiritual abuse

Many women fall prey to domestic abuse, domestic violence or both each year, but domestic violence, however, is the most dangerous as it can possibly lead to the murder of the victim.

The difference between domestic abuse and domestic violence

Domestic abuse: This is referred to as spousal abuse. It occurs when someone emotionally involved in a relationship or marriage attempts to dominate the other person or exercise control by the misuse of power.

This consists of a more subtle action or behaviour, in the form of verbal or non-verbal abuse, emotional abuse, psychological abuse and mental abuse.

It is a hidden crime, which is not only disregarded as a crime, but also excluded from statistics. On the other hand, the fact that it is not treated as a crime does not mean that it is not serious. It is invisible to the eye, as one cannot see it, but is usually a lot worse than physical abuse as the scars can be deep.

Survivors often find this form of abuse more destructive as it is likely that the damage done may also affect the victim's state of mind. Hence, the classic verse *'Sticks and stones may break my bones, but bullying and name-calling can emotionally scar me forever'*, or rather, it seems that *'broken bones will heal far more quicker than a battered soul.'*

Being able to recognise the early signs of abuse is the first step towards seeking help or doing something about it. This form of abuse usually escalates from non-verbal to verbal abuse, from threatening behaviour and then on to violence. Although physical violation may be the most obvious danger, the emotional and psychological consequences of domestic abuse are often very severe.

The following are some different forms of domestic abuse by the abuser:

Criticism, instillation of fear, intimidation, harassment, degradation, isolation, spying, blame, swearing, yelling, ridiculing, humiliation, embarrassment, lack of trust, rejection, abandonment, interrogation, restrictions, house entrapment and the constant mockery of their victim.

These methods of abuse can affect the victim both emotionally and negatively. They often lead to the development of stress, depression, low levels of insecurity, lack of confidence, very low self-esteem, lack of self-worth, feelings of being unloved, loneliness, anxiety, diminished mental and physical health.

Recognising an abusive situation is the first step towards breaking free and when this reality is acknowledged, it then becomes a lot easier to seek the appropriate help required.

The effects on the victim of domestic abuse are normally psychological, emotional or mental. Professional help such as counselling or seeking appropriate help from a caring and trustworthy friend, neighbour or family member may help. In addition, as the victim, safely removing one's self from the situation can often go a long way in helping or preventing any further damage that could possibly be long- term.

Domestic abuse that involves any physical action or force is known as domestic violence.

Domestic violence: This occurs when the abuser uses excessive force or inflicts a physical injury by one family or household member on another. It can also be a repeated or habitual pattern of such behaviour.

Family violence often includes wife abuse, child abuse, elderly abuse and other violent acts between family members. Wife beating or battering are typical cases of domestic violence.

Domestic violence is prevalent, serious and detrimental to one's health. It is also criminal, breaks up families, ruins lives and has a lasting impact on the people affected. Although it has been in existence for decades, it has only been taken seriously as a criminal issue in the last ten years and its elimination is not within sight. Prior to that, most of the cases were brushed under the carpet and regarded as *just a domestic.*

This physical form of abuse may often include some of the following acts carried out on their victim: hitting, punching, throwing, biting, pushing, pinching, burning, choking, kicking, stalking, restraining, confinement, sexual assault, slapping, grabbing, beating, tripping, battering, bruising, shaking, holding, breaking bones, assaulting with a weapon such as a knife, hammer or gun.

The long-term effects of domestic violence may often lead to most effects suffered from domestic abuse, but may in due course end in more serious health problems, such as panic attacks, traumatic stress disorder, insomnia, disability, permanent injury, actual or grievous bodily harm, substance abuse, fatality or the murder of the victim.

Financial abuse: This is another form of abuse, whereby the abuser leaves the victim almost penniless or financially broke. The victim may also be prevented from buying the bare necessities such as food, toiletries, clothing, or even medication, often being refused the right to earn their own money or the privilege of choosing their own profession. The abuser may also go as far as stealing whatever money or assets the victim may have acquired, for their own personal gain. The reason behind this is usually for the ownership, control, possession and the total dependency of the victim on the abuser.

Stalking: This type of abuse is generally classed as a form of domestic violence. It has now become a criminal offence in England and Wales. This occurs when the victim tries to sever all ties with their abuser, but the abuser still succeeds in instilling fear in the victim by monitoring their whereabouts.

There is the possibility that the stalker may harm or seek revenge because the victim has left them. This may lead them to carry out serious threats or even death threats against the victim and their family, destroying their personal property, watching or recording the victim with either a hidden camera or video recorder or sending unwanted gifts.

Cyber Stalking: This is another form of abuse, but the stalking is done over the Internet. Nevertheless, both forms of stalking are dangerous and may eventually lead to any form of unpredictable violence in the end.

Sexual and physical violence: These are often linked, as they usually go hand in hand with one another. There is every tendency for an abuser who is physically violent towards their spouse to also become sexually abusive and it often consists of some or all of the following:

Sexual assault or rape: This occurs when the abuser forces their partner or victim to have unwanted sex with them. The abuser gains control over their victim by way of sexual harassment and may force the victim to watch or perform home pornography. This forceful or degrading act is referred to as sexual exploitation.

Spiritual abuse: This is a form of abuse where the abuser mocks their victim's religious beliefs. They may even force their children to be raised with a different religion in order to punish or hurt the victim's feelings.

Almost every dysfunction in life stems from the family. A home is the first place of learning for a child. Domestic violence is predominantly a learned behaviour, whereby the abuser may have been abused by someone during childhood, or may have witnessed abuse as a child in the household they were brought up in. For example, a child's exposure to a father's abuse of a mother is the major risk factor for transmitting domestic violence from one generation to the next.

This cycle of domestic violence is difficult to break because some parents have presented violence as the norm. It is also common behaviour and a norm in some countries. People living with domestic violence in their households often believe that violence is the only way to vent anger.

Domestic violence and the other forms of abuse are mainly due to the abuser being power and control driven. In most cases, it is not just about wanting it, but also about needing it in order to feel a false sense of self-worth. The actual truth may be that they probably suffer from very low self-esteem to behave in such a manner.

The abuser's character is somewhat confusing in the sense that they will normally deceive or present themselves to the public as charming and fantastic people. In many situations, they tend to behave in a very different way from what they are truly like towards their victim, that it would be almost impossible for any outsider to believe if the truth were told.

Both their private and public lives are different. The character displayed by the abuser is usually similar to the two split personalities of *Dr Jekyll and Mr Hyde.* This is also known as multiple personality disorder, a condition that causes a person to display two personalities that are each very noticeable. The victim or other members of a household are more than likely to be the only people that have the privilege of witnessing the horrible, dark and abusive side of the abuser.

The truth is that many victims are not aware of the fact that they are being abused. They seem to think that it is only when it gets physical that an abuse has occurred, which is so untrue.

A number of causes that can trigger or set off most domestic violence are provocation, desperation, depression, anger, financial hardship, stress *(one of the biggest causes of all relationship problems),* drugs and alcohol, which may sometimes be used as an excuse, sexual jealousy, possessiveness, substance abuse and mental illness.

Other known factors are the misuse of power, sense of entitlement and gaining control rather than lack of it.

The effects of domestic violence on children

The greatest gift a parent can give any child under their care is to keep them safe and free from any abusive situation or environment.

Children who live in a house where abuse occurs or who witness domestic violence are indirect victims and may often develop serious behavioural, emotional, developmental or academic problems. There is a tendency that they may also become violent themselves by acting up at home or school, while others do the complete opposite by striving to become perfect children. It is also possible for children from such abusive environments to develop low self-esteem or to suffer from depression.

In their later years, such adults, who were exposed to domestic violence in their household as children and teens, may possess the following tendencies:

- Attempt or commit suicide
- Use violence in the community or at school in response to a perceived threat
- Use violence to enhance their reputation and self-esteem
- Use drugs

- Offend by bullying, commit crimes such as sexual assault
- Become abusers in their own relationships later in life

A cluster of the following are warning signs of domestic abuse:

There are numerous signs of an abusive relationship, but one of the first tell tale signs is fear or being nervous of your partner. The feeling of having to walk on eggshells around your partner and constantly watching your tongue or what you say so as not to upset him. There is every chance that this kind of situation in a relationship is abusive and unhealthy.

Other signs of an abusive relationship may include:

- Being constantly belittled by a partner
- Control
- Feelings of self-loathing
- Helplessness
- Desperation
- Constant outburst of tears, crying
- Bruises and other signs of impact on the skin, with the excuse of *accidents*
- Harassing phone calls
- Depression
- Isolation from friends and family
- Insufficient resources to live on, always broke, *(lack of money, credit cards, car)*
- Victim having to constantly apologise

- Hyper-vigilance: This happens when a victim is constantly tense, on guard and always scanning the environment looking to identify potential sources of threat or danger. They tend to startle easily, such as *being jumpy* at any unexpected noise or sound. This is often accompanied by changes in behaviour, such as choosing to sit in the far corner of a room, always being on the lookout and being very aware of all exits. At extreme levels, hyperactive vigilance may appear similar to paranoia.

The cycle

The cycle of abuse is vicious and difficult to break, as a lot of women have either experienced violence in the form of discipline, chastisement or beatings from their parents as children. A family friend or family member may also have sexually molested some people.

Patterns of abuse

- Abuser threatens violence
- Abuser strikes
- Abuser apologises, promises to change and offers gifts
- The cycle repeats itself
- Eventually, the violence becomes more frequent and severe over time

Breaking the cycle of abuse

The only way to break the cycle of abuse is to shatter the abuse patterns for good:

Take action, leave – NOW, rather than later.

Tell someone you can trust.

Survivor

A person who continues to function or prosper in spite of opposition, hardship or setbacks.

A survivor is also a former victim who eventually faced the facts and accepted that it was impossible to change either the abuser or the relationship, but instead chose to commit to turning their own life round for the better.

An immense amount of thought would have gone into acknowledging their abusive situation, for the survivor to have realised that they were not doing themselves any favours by remaining in the abusive relationship. They would have strived to either stop the abuse or to remove themselves from the abusive relationship.

Therefore, the point at which the victim says *No, enough is enough,* and refuses to be a victim any longer, makes a commitment to break free by moving on; putting it all behind them and not giving up, is when they have reached the *decisive moment* in their lives. This indeed is a significant *turning point* for the victim who then becomes a *survivor.*

Surviving, however, means a lot more than just having endured the previous verbal, mental, emotional and physical abuse. It also means being free from the emotional bondage of your abuser and moving on to a safer option or lifestyle. It is not always easy, but much better than waiting for the next episode of violence or constantly walking on eggshells in an abusive relationship.

You own your life and have the power of freedom, which is the ability to make your own choices rather than having someone else make them for you. A survivor would have learnt some valuable lessons and life experiences along the way, among which should include an awareness of being unable to change the impossible. Above all, the most important and priceless gifts are having your sanity intact and the joy of being alive!

Some survivors often tend to take what knowledge and experience they have, no matter how vast or small, to share with people, or offer their services voluntarily in order to help or reach out to other victims.

★ ★ ★

Please note that I am not a counsellor, neither do I possess any qualifications in this field, apart from being a former victim. Thankfully, I am now a victor and a survivor. The information is based on my knowledge, personal experiences and some research that I carried out. It is, therefore, neither comprehensive nor flawless, but it will do you no harm!

A Blog From an Ex-fashionista

A blog about my previous life in the fashion industry, redundancy, motherhood, politics, society and my plans for the future.

Domestic Violence: Why doesn't she just leave? Posted on January 28, 2012 by Ex-fashionista.

Warning: If you have been a victim of domestic violence, the following may trigger memories that you would prefer not to re-live. Please be prepared that this is a possibility before reading further. I do not want to cause any unnecessary distress. Many thanks.

If there is one sentence guaranteed to cause me to feel absolute rage, it is "why doesn't she just leave?" in relation to domestic violence. My initial thought, however, is one of envy. Clearly, the person uttering these words has never experienced or witnessed domestic violence – they are one of the lucky ones. I could bombard you with statistics here, such as 1 in 4 women experience domestic violence in their lifetime, or on average 2 women a week are killed by a current or former partner, or a particularly horrifying one, courtesy of the

Department for Health; at least 750,000 children a week in the UK witness domestic violence.

If you are interested in further statistics and analysis, I highly recommend the summary document produced by Women's Aid. (www.womensaid.org.uk).

Statistics aside, domestic violence is a hidden crime so I accept that it is unrealistic to expect those who lack personal experience of it to fully understand. Consequently, while ignorant observations and simplifications make me angry, I appreciate that they are precisely that, ignorant. So, I thought I'd have a go at trying to de-mystify domestic violence for those with no experience of it. If this blog helps one person to understand and not ask the dreaded question, I figure it's worth writing.

Domestic violence rarely happens overnight or right at the beginning of a relationship, although evidence suggests that domestic violence is common in relationships that progress to the "living-in" stage quickly. There is usually a build up of abusive behaviour over time, which can range from weeks to years and the forerunner to physical abuse is usually emotional abuse. There is no "type" of person that is abused; it can happen to literally anyone, including the most confident and outgoing of your family and friends. Domestic violence is a type of control, which is why it doesn't happen over night; other types of controlling behaviour usually precede it. At the start of a relationship, someone calling excessively to chat, or showing a little jealousy when you get dressed up to go out for a night with your friends can be flattering rather than concerning. Jealous incidents can easily be written off as a natural part of loving someone. Imagine if your new partner showed a lot of interest in your new hair style or your latest shopping expedition. Surely, most people would be flattered to have a partner that was so attentive. I should probably point out here that not all men or women that demonstrate this kind of behaviour are potential abusers, far from it. However, I think it's important to show how these types of behaviour can link together over time to build a much bigger picture of abuse.

So once the relationship is established, behaviour may progress, and where a partner used to take interest in your new hair style they now criticise it or tell you they prefer it a different way. Where they once called you regularly because they missed you, they now call to check exactly where you are and who you are with. When you dress up for a night out he might tell you not to wear that dress because it's too low cut or say your skirt is too short and he doesn't want "his" girlfriend dressing like that. Or perhaps when you arrange to have a night out without him, he starts sulking and complaining about it. Alternatively, he goes out drinking for the night and when he comes home he's verbally abusive or threatening but in the morning he acts as if nothing happened, blames it on the alcohol or apologises profusely and promises that it won't ever happen again. If you love someone, it's easy to forgive these things at first and if you have no experience of abuse, why would you start to link this kind of behaviour together and realise how it can progress?

Emotional abuse can have a profound effect and more often than not it is a pre-cursor to physical abuse.

Imagine being told you are fat, ugly, useless, stupid, that nobody else will want you and that everybody hates you over and over again, day in, day out. Also, consistently being isolated from your family and friends because you don't "need anybody else" so your support network begins to crumble (assuming you had one to begin with). Family and friends may well feel rejected or hurt because they don't realise what is happening to you and perceive you to be choosing to spend time with your partner over them. Thus, they make themselves less approachable. That in itself is enough to destroy even the strongest person and make them believe that everything that they are being told about themselves is true. If you then add physical violence to the existing emotional abuse, is it any wonder if someone feels helpless and ashamed? Physical violence, when it first happens, usually comes as a shock, which is why when a perpetrator appears to show utter remorse, a victim believes it won't happen again. In reality, it almost always happens again and once that initial barrier has been broken, it tends to get progressively worse. Ask yourself, if someone was threatening to harm or kill you, your children or your family if you dared to report or leave them, would you do it?

If someone is consistently violent towards you, you know what they are capable of, so it really isn't a huge leap to believe them when they say that they will kill or seriously injure you. If they threaten to take your children away or kill them if you leave, why wouldn't you believe that they will do it? If they say that if you leave them they will find you no matter where you go, why wouldn't you think that is exactly what they will do?

Domestic violence, like other forms of abuse, thrives on secrecy. The perpetrator relies on the fact that the consequences that they will suffer if they report the abuse are so severe that the victim will not tell anyone what is happening to them. This is incredibly powerful. Personally, this is why I feel escaping the situation is paramount and reporting the crime is secondary. I know I may well get berated for saying that but safety is far more important than retribution in my view. I would, however, urge any victim to visit their doctor in absolute confidence and show them the physical signs of abuse when they occur. That way there is documentary evidence that can be used at a later date as necessary. I'm not in any way suggesting that domestic violence isn't a crime or that it shouldn't be reported, it is and it should be. I'm simply saying that in many situations, having someone convicted or arrested for it is not the most pressing concern, survival is.

Not everyone has somewhere to go. They may be too scared to go to family or friends in case it puts them at risk from the abuser too. They may also worry that they have no money or means of financial support, making them feel utterly trapped. It is common for abusers to take total control of financial concerns and also place debt, i.e. loans and credit cards in their victim's name. When people question why women don't leave, this is the kind of factor that they do not consider. In times of recession and huge cuts to welfare, the financial considerations involved in trying to leave become even more poignant. The other factor that is often underestimated is fear. Fear will affect every single thought an abused person has and every single decision that they make. Combine this with feelings of embarrassment and shame and you have a maelstrom of emotions that make rational thought almost impossible.

If you are reading this and you are the victim of abuse or know someone who is, please do not despair, there are ways out and people that can help. Both Refuge and Women's Aid offer excellent support and advice. They can help a victim formulate a plan to leave and advise them on sources of financial support and places that they can go to. This includes safe houses if a victim is frightened about being followed or found. These organisations realise that the path to leaving may be a long one and that a victim will only do so when they have the strength and they are ready. They do not judge, they merely offer support and advice for how to stay safe while still living with an abuser, as well as advice on the steps to take to help you leave safely and effectively. They can also offer support if you are concerned about a friend or family member. When you are in the midst of domestic violence it feels like a very lonely business, but you are not alone. It is a common occurrence and 25% of the women you will ever meet have experienced it in some form. It is not your fault; it is your abuser's fault.

If you are reading this and you do not have any experience of domestic violence, I hope I have opened your eyes to it just a little. If you have ever questioned in the past why someone didn't leave an abuser I hope that in the future you will not judge, but try to understand why leaving isn't nearly as easy as you first thought.

I have literally only scratched the surface of this subject here and I do intend to write further on the topic of domestic violence in the future.

Statistics On Domestic Violence & Abuse

Women's Aid states that:

'1 in 4 women will be a victim of domestic violence in their lifetime – many of these on a number of occasions.'

'1 incident of domestic violence is reported to the police every minute.'

'On average, 2 women a week are killed by a current or former male partner.'

Clare's Law

"Domestic Violence Disclosure Scheme - Government announces one-year pilot from summer 2012.

On 5 March 2012, the government announced that a one-year pilot would take place from the summer of 2012 to test out a domestic violence disclosure scheme in the police force areas of Greater Manchester, Gwent, Nottinghamshire and Wiltshire. The pilot will test a process to enable the police to disclose to the public information about previous violent offending by a new or existing partner where this may help protect them from further violent offending. The government is committed to ensuring that the police and other agencies have the tools necessary to tackle domestic violence to bring offenders to justice and to ensure victims have the support they need to rebuild their lives.

Domestic violence is unacceptable and tackling the issue is a priority for this government."

References

Every woman and child experiencing domestic violence has different needs. There is no single package of services to meet these needs and there is no such thing as 'one size fits all.'

There are a number of organisations available, which offer support to vulnerable victims of domestic violence or abuse. Some of these are listed below:

Women's Aid

In Chiswick, London, 1971, Erin Pizzey formed a social meeting place for women who wanted to make a difference in their local communities. It had absolutely nothing to do with domestic violence until a bruised woman coincidentally asked for its help, since there was no one else to help her.

As a group of feminist charities across the UK and the world's first Domestic Violence Shelter, its aim is to end domestic violence against women and children, and the policy is *no-one should ever be turned away,* which is known as the *open door* policy.

The organisation works at all levels to ensure women's safety, it helps to prevent the reoccurrence of domestic violence and runs a free phone service 24 hours a day.

Contact: 0808 2000 247

Refuge

This is a shelter or temporary place of refuge where battered women and their children can go for protection from their abusers. There is a network of refuges across the country that provides emergency accommodation for women fleeing abuse. They offer a lot more than just a roof over the heads of victims of domestic violence. The victims are given the opportunity to make decisions regarding their future and a number of specialist refuge staff members are available to provide emotional and practical support. Contact: 0800 200 0247

Refuge offers a range of services, which gives the victims access to professional support regardless of their situation, among which include:

National Domestic Violence Helpline

A free-phone 24-hour National Domestic Violence Helpline, run in partnership with Women's Aid. It is open 24 hours a day, every single day and the helpline workers are available to offer emotional support and practical information to help women explore their options in order to escape the abuse. Contact: 0800 200247

Independent Legal Advocacy

Independent Domestic Violence Advocacy or Adviser (IDVA) is a government initiative introduced to reduce the number of domestic-related homicides, but focuses more on high-risk clients. They also provide expert guidance for women going through civil and criminal courts, help women to obtain non-molestation injunctions, occupation orders and help increase conviction rates. Contact numbers: 01744 743 200/01274 667104

Outreach Services

Some women may choose not to go into a refuge or to leave their homes. Outreach Services' workers meet with women at safe times in their own homes or at a discreet place in the community. They help women to draw up safety plans, process housing applications and provide emotional support.

Stop Abuse for Everyone (SAFE)

This is a registered charity, which provides refuge and support services through its Outreach Team for people of all ages.

Contact: 01392 667144 or call free on 0800 328 3070

The Relationships Centre

This is a registered charity. The centre offers support to families with relationship problems, the survivors of abuse or individuals seeking to make their lives more positive and independent. The Relationships Centre (Cheshire) Limited (registered Company in England & Wales No. 05173755) is a wholly owned subsidiary and trades on behalf of the Relationships Centre.

The Relationships Centre within the context of this Privacy Policy means both organisations and there are services available throughout the North West. They can be contacted using the details below:

Tel: 01925 246910

Fax: 01925 246920

Email: info@therelationshipscentre.co.uk

Youth Counselling Services

This helpline number 0808 808 8000, is for the counselling services and they are available to offer support to young people between the ages of 11 and 25.

The Men's Advice Line

The Men's Advice Line offers support for male victims of domestic violence.

Help-lines: 0800 801 0327/0800 801 0327

Visit the website: www.mensadviceline.org.uk

Mankind Initiative

0182 333 4244

Mankind.org.uk

Help and support

Bliss, the charity for newborns

Helpline: 0500 618 140

www.bliss.org.uk

Premature babies:
http://www.dailymail.co.uk/femail/article-93556/Premature-birth.htmlixzz21r9P3Inw

Emotional Abuse: The Victim and Abuser
http://www.drphil.com/articles/article/19/

EX-FASHIONISTA http://www.exfashionista.co.uk

Renée Matthews website: www.reneematthews.co.uk

Acknowledgements

My sweet mother, Mrs Jayne Orobosa Ugowe, you did not bring me into this world to suffer at the hands of anyone, and no doubt it broke your precious heart to watch me go through what I did. However, I am glad you are alive to see that I am currently a happy woman, because I heeded your advice. I want to take this opportunity to let you know how much I appreciate you, for you are my rock, my best friend and my confidante. My prayer request each day is for God to bless your every minute, to brighten your every day and to enrich you with good health and a long life. In the next life, if fate allows our paths to cross, I would choose you as my mother in a heartbeat, *my beautiful Lady Jayne.* On behalf of my Dad, my siblings, our spouses and our children, I would like to thank you for loving us and for constantly putting us all first. You are indeed our queen of hearts who we treasure, honour and try to emulate. We love you sincerely Mum, God bless you.

My dear Dad, the Honourable Matthew Omoregie Ugowe, thank you for your love and care, for I know you love us all in your own special way. Thank you for your hard work, time and continued effort over the years. I appreciate you for helping me get better while I was poorly as a child and for the discipline, morals and values you instilled in me. Collectively, they helped shape my character during my formative years and although your methods of discipline were extreme at times, they have kept me grounded to date. May God continually grant you good health and long life, Daddy. I love you.

★ ★ ★

My most sincere gratitude to the following special people and businesses:

Tom Matthews, Jamie Matthews, Christine Edugie Asumu, Gloria Ugowe-Ajim, Michelle Ugowe-Anyia, Maxwell Ugowe-Matthews, Geraldine Ugowe, Michael Ugowe, Mayor Anna Mbachu, Cllr. Jane Brophy, Cllr. Sue McGuire, Chris Davies MEP, Cllr. Neil and Sandra Taylor, Hilary Stephenson, Preference Iyen-Sullivan, Belief Ranney, Uyi Iyen, Osaretin Iyen, Godsgift Iyen, Uwaila Kim Owie, Nicola Doherty, Sarah Connelly, Matthew & Susannah Walker, Mike & Janet Lee, Adeshola Saka-Salami a.k.a. Hollywoodmamamia, Prince Afolabi Dave Obasuyi, Emmanuel & Nihinlolawa Ebagua, Edna Ejemhen Ewalefoh Ehizokhale, Frances Dupe Lawal, Mercy Ayoola Johnson, Sammy & Falisandra Badmus, Omatsola & Nonye Barrow, Pat & Dele Ojutalayo, Omosefe Asemota Aguaze, Ebitimi Torubiri Ikwuazom, Sarena Johnson, Osasogie Erhabor, Don Asumu, Segun Johnson Ajim, Miss R.E.B. Howard, Diana Rogers, Andy Malone, Michelle Bailey, Issac &

Felicia Omoruyi, Majeck & Pastor Dorah Kuyoro, Leanne Burton, Bolanle Alogba, Edward Erhabor, Michael Lee, Carol Oseghale, Lady Dr Addy Lazz-Onyenobi & Sir Dr Lazz-Onyenobi, Orobosa Ebagua, Grace Edoimioya, Eghosa Erhabor, Israel & Rose Umweni, Deacon & Mrs. Osunde, Pastor Christy Ede Oziengbe, Sonja Salcido (Arizona), Josephine Kziuik, Anthonia Ugowe, Mercy Igbinosa, Esther Osawe, Mick Adams, Rosemary Casey, Princess Seun, David & Anita Adams, Tina Ifaluyi, Gloria Nosa, Titilola Aboyade-Cole, Hon. & Mrs. Buba Douglas (Verona), Clara Olatunji, Margaret Lee, Mr. & Mrs. Victor Igbinovia, Dale Rochford, Suzan Osemwegie, Omoruyi Osamogie, Osato Salami, Mr. & Mrs. Godwin Osa-Osagie, Theophilus & Hilary Asumu, Commissioner Patrick Ugowe, Mr. & Mrs. Oboh, Kenny Oboh, Bose Konkon, Adrian Morgan, Mrs Izah, Larry & Nike Allen, Dr Constant & Marie Nwoji, Paul Obasogie, Chris Femi Davies, Frank & Patricia Omorodion, Regina Uanseru, Marilyn Morgan, Fatima Ohonbamu, Betty Nwabunike, Godwin & Sandra Aghayere, Getty Ewone-Jegede, Bridget Omogiate, Efosa Ugowe, Joy Obaze, Auntie Bridget, Rose Ugowe, Clara Ugheoke Emuekpere, Mr. & Mrs. Anthony Ugowe, Debbie Taylor Ninnis, Sandra Downings, Patience Obanor, Sandra Otobo, Aubrey Sutton, Lian Staley Jackson, Henry Okhuevbie, Abayomi Yomi, Temitope Ajayi, Mrs. Erhumwunse, Irene Uboma, Oge Uboma, Mr & Mrs Keith Latham, Idowu Ehigie, Helen Omoroghowan, Ota Uwaifo, Jan Oye, Mr. & Mrs. Awopetu, Mr. & Mrs. Barrow (Chicago) Linda Barrow Ikponmwosa, Grace Edobor, Emmanuel Onyemeziem, Joyce Aghedo, Esther Okuonghae, Wendy Taylor, Aunty Victoria, Debbie Broughton, Monday

Obasohan, Clement Adomokhai, Karen Taylor, Belinda Oke-Ugbaje, Sam & Edna Omigie, Blessing Ifaluyi, Hilton Idahosa, Oluwabunmi Joseph, John Adams, Kyle Ford, Adrienne Kilburn, Philip Butterfield, Efe Idemudia, Hameed Majidi, Tina Imonikhe, Joy Jasper, Chief Bimbo Roberts Folayan *(Chair,* Central Association of Nigerians in the UK *CANUK),* Canon Adrian M. Rhodes *(President* of the European Association for Psychotherapy *EAP*), Canon Andrew Shanks *(Theologian),* Modus Visual Media Limited, Mr & Mrs Steven Woods, Tex & Christiana Ogbomo, Sammy Johnson, Billy Igbinosa, Teeplus Events, Sheena Macleod, Dorlapoh Crystals, Patricio & Judith Joao, Amber Makhdoom, Pastor Philip Oluwole Ukanah, Mrs Hannah Eke *(Nigerian High Commission)* Mary Peters, Marika Buttigieg, Ex-fashionista, Women's Aid UK, Jewish Women's Aid and Dr. Phil *(USA).* My half brothers and all the members of the Ugowe/Matthews Clan, I love you all.

The Dearly Departed

Mr. & Mrs. Peter Ugowe, Mr. & Mrs. Josiah Erhabor, Mr. & Mrs. Pius Ugowe, Tom & Kathleen, Uncle Jack, Uncle Morris, Emmanuel Ugowe, Mr. Aigbi, Uncle Anthony, Tony Owens, Mrs Omoruyi, Auntie Vero, Abel Okunbor, Pa Isaiah Ehigie, Roy Downings, Rawson Hayble, Mrs. Irene Hadfield and Sir Clement Obiora Akpamgbo.

Adieu! Not only will your memories live on and make me smile forever; you shall also be missed but never forgotten. May your gentle souls rest in peace, amen!